Nurturing Life Skills to Empower Your Elementary Child

Includes Developmental Milestones, Fundamental Skills, Motivational Strategies, and Practical Exercises

Mari L. Ann

Dedicated to my family,

*to my children who have taught me the meaning of unconditional love
and to my husband who encourages me through life.*

Contents

Introduction

Parenting is an incredible journey filled with boundless love, moments of pure insanity, and the joy of watching your child grow and thrive. It's a journey that challenges, teaches, and reshapes you as much as it does your child. No matter how seasoned or new to the role, we all face the same big parenting question at some point: "How do I prepare my child for the world ahead?" You are not alone.

Every parent understands that our children's future success depends on more than just academic knowledge. We want our kids to become responsible, confident, and resilient individuals who can adapt to life's ever-changing landscape. The elementary school curriculum is heavily weighted toward subjects like mathematics, language arts, and science, which are undoubtedly necessary. However, the emphasis on these subjects often means that crucial life skills are overlooked. Skills such as communication, empathy, decision-making, household management, and financial literacy are relegated to the sidelines or left to be developed at home, often without clear guidance for parents. Young adults are graduating high school and even college without a fundamental understanding of personal finance, emotional intelligence, or the ability to navigate the complexities of adult life independently. This lack of preparation often results in frustration, anxiety, and a sense of unpreparedness among young people.

The rise of helicopter parenting, driven by fears of potential dangers and societal pressures, has inadvertently hindered our children's development of self-reliance. We want to protect them from harm and shield them from failure, but in doing so, we unintentionally deprive them of the skills they need to flourish. We often overprotect and micromanage our children's lives, stifling their growth and independence. Let's face it, sometimes, it's just easier for us to do things because we don't always have the time and patience to let our kids do things on their own. By providing them with necessary life skills and relinquishing control, we can foster their self-confidence and equip them with the tools to navigate the challenges that lie ahead.

Parents are their children's first teachers, and their guidance plays a vital role in shaping their character and abilities. Having children grow in confidence, resilience, and empathy is an undeniable positive change. How can we effectively nurture life skills in our children, providing an environment that encourages development while navigating the busy demands of modern life?

Drawing from my experiences as a parent and an educator, I have spent years researching and studying the most effective techniques and strategies to impart essential life skills to young learners. I consulted experts, researched educational methods, and gathered insights from experienced parents. Within these pages, we will embark on a comprehensive exploration of developmental milestones, age-appropriate essential life skills, their significance, and how you can effectively use strategies and exercises to make a tangible difference in your child's life.

This book is a practical guide tailored for busy parents, filled with actionable advice, real-life examples, and interactive exercises. It's designed to empower you, the parent, to become your child's guide on their journey to acquiring essential life skills. We will explore a treasure trove of life skills that will empower your child not only to navigate the path ahead but also to flourish on it. These life skills are not abstract concepts but practical tools that can be nurtured, developed, and woven into your child's everyday life.

By the time you finish reading this book, you will have:

1. **Understanding:** You will know what life skills are, why they are essential, how they contribute to your child's well-rounded development, and have a guideline on when and how to introduce new skills based on your child's age and milestones.
2. **Practical Strategies:** You will have a toolkit of practical strategies and activities to nurture specific life skills in your child, from emotional intelligence to financial literacy.
3. **Confidence:** You will feel confident in your ability to guide your child's growth and development, even in the face of life's challenges.
4. **Stronger Bonds:** You will strengthen your relationship with your child through shared experiences and open communication, fostering trust and understanding.
5. **Better Prepared Kids:** Most importantly, you will empower your child with the skills they need to face the future with resilience, adaptability, and independence.

Our collective goal is to create an environment where children not only excel academically but also become compassionate, confident, and capable individuals, ready to tackle the challenges and opportunities that life presents. So, whether you're a seasoned parent looking to enhance your child's skill set or a new parent eager to embark on this incredible journey of growth and learning, you've come to the right place. Together, we will unlock the potential within your child, fostering qualities that will not only prepare them for the future but also empower them to embrace the present with confidence and enthusiasm. Let's begin this transformative journey of empowerment, growth, and independence. Let us prepare our children to thrive in the ever-changing world.

Chapter 1

Essential Life Skills for Elementary Kids

L ife skills are practical knowledge used in real day-to-day life. Essential abilities and competencies help us navigate and thrive in various aspects of our lives. The learned skills, along with our character and values, enable us to handle daily challenges, take on more responsibilities, make informed decisions, and interact effectively with others. Often interrelated, the cognitive, social, emotional, and physical skills are learned in tandem.

For elementary school kids, developing a solid foundation in life skills is crucial as it sets the stage for their future growth and success. It's essential to make the learning process enjoyable and age-appropriate. Especially for elementary-aged children, using games, songs, and visual aids helps reinforce skills. Additionally, modeling as parents and caregivers sets a strong example for children to follow. By teaching these skills early on, you are helping your child develop life-long healthy habits.

The primary years should focus on establishing awareness, developing interpersonal relationships, their ability to cope with emotions, and building their stamina. All of which will also reinforce their competency for more vital study skills in their academic life. Here are eleven of the most essential life skills for elementary school kids:

1. **Communication:** Communication skills involve expressing oneself clearly and effectively verbally and non-verbally. It includes active listening, expressing thoughts and feelings, and understanding body language. Good communication skills help children build relationships, resolve conflicts, and collaborate with others.

2. **Problem-solving:** Problem-solving skills teach children how to think critically, analyze situations, and find creative solutions. Encouraging kids to identify problems, break them down into smaller parts, and brainstorm possible solutions helps them become resourceful and adaptable.

3. **Decision-making:** Decision-making skills involve evaluating options, considering consequences, and making choices based on values and priorities. Teaching children to make informed decisions empowers them to take responsibility for their actions and builds their confidence.

4. **Empathy:** Empathy is the ability to understand and share the feelings of others. It helps children develop positive relationships, show compassion, and resolve conflicts peacefully. Encouraging kids to consider others' perspectives and practice kindness nurtures empathy.

5. **Emotional intelligence:** Emotional intelligence involves recognizing and managing one's own emotions (anger, stress, anxiety), as well as understanding and responding to the emotions of others. Teaching kids to identify and regulate their emotions fosters self-awareness, empathy, and healthy relationships.

6. **Time management:** Time management skills help children prioritize tasks, set goals, and use their time effectively. Teaching kids to organize their time and develop routines empowers them to be responsible, meet deadlines, and balance their activities.

7. **Collaboration:** Collaboration skills involve working effectively with others, sharing responsibilities, and respecting diverse opinions. Encouraging teamwork, active participation, and communication in group activities helps

kids develop social skills and build cooperative relationships.

8. **Adaptability:** Adaptability refers to the ability to adjust to new situations, handle change, and embrace challenges. Teaching children to be flexible, open-minded, and resilient empowers them to navigate uncertainties and learn from setbacks.

9. **Self-confidence:** Self-confidence is the belief in one's abilities and worth. Fostering a positive self-image, celebrating achievements, and encouraging kids to take risks helps build their self-esteem and resilience.

10. **Critical thinking:** Critical thinking skills involve analyzing information, questioning assumptions, and making informed judgments. Encouraging curiosity, problem-solving, and exploring different perspectives helps children develop independent thinking skills.

11. **Healthy hygiene:** Healthy hygiene skills include establishing and maintaining self-care routines. Help kids form good habits early on for longevity and avoid some, not all, illnesses.

12. **Physical training:** Physical training promotes physical fitness and the development of essential motor skills and helps children maintain an active lifestyle.

By focusing on developing these life skills, elementary school kids can lay a strong foundation for their personal growth, social interactions, and academic success. No one wants to be lectured to. Instead, integrate the skills into everyday activities and experiences. Many skills are interrelated and can be learned in tandem with household chores, financial literacy, and team sports. Kids learn best by example!

This life skills book is a guideline structured by grades that generally coincide with age. However, we all learn at different paces, and later on, I'll talk more about developmental milestones that should also be considered. We all have diverse backgrounds, and you know your child best. Take into account your child's level of maturity and abilities. Some skills will come naturally, while others will need more practice. Find your child's strengths and lean into areas needing improvement. The formative years are when we must build a strong foundation of skills for achieving the right mindset and actions to accomplish goals.

Chapter 2

The ABC'S - Aware, Brave, Care & Strong

We can further break down the main four areas of elementary life skills from cognitive, social, emotional, and physical into the ABC'S of life skills:

Aware: Kids start off living in their own bubble. It takes time for them to be cognitive of the world around them and how they are able to interact with it. As their world expands, young children must learn how to navigate their situational awareness using cognitive skills. They start observing their surroundings more carefully and gather information, becoming familiar with certain people, places, and routines. This establishes what's normal for them.

As they grow older and have more experiences, they will be able to make predictions based on their observations, allowing them to detect a potential risk or danger. As they become more aware, they will use their self-directed critical thinking, problem-solving, and decision-making skills. By learning to predict the outcome of their decisions/actions, they can think of alternative solutions and have more favorable consequences from their choices. They can learn to map out solutions into manageable steps.

Give your child opportunities to explore their surroundings, encouraging curiosity and fostering open communication. Help them develop the skills to assess and respond to situations effectively. They will also develop social awareness by reading social cues, considering the emotions of those around them, and adapting their behavior accordingly.

Brave: Social skills for children allow them to effectively interact with others, build relationships, and navigate social situations. For some, it's a gradual process to come out of their little shell, and for others, they just naturally enjoy being social but need to be dialed back some. Interpersonal interactions and communication skills can be uncomfortable and require children to step out of their comfort zone. To be brave is to be courageous ready to face or endure uncomfortable situations.

Children learn cooperation by sharing, taking turns, and compromising. Teach your child how to express their needs and boundaries without being aggressive or passive. Naturally social people may need to work on respecting personal space and boundaries. All kids need to be equipped with social skills so they can resolve conflicts peacefully and constructively, reducing the likelihood of altercations or misunderstandings. Teach tolerance and acceptance by respecting differences in others and fostering inclusivity. Children with strong social skills are more likely to be resilient in the face of bullying and better equipped to seek help when needed.

Kids need to learn how to initiate and build friendships, including approaching others, starting conversations, and finding common interests. Understanding and using appropriate body language, such as eye contact and facial expressions, is vital for effective non-verbal communication. It may seem like common sense, but as digital interactions are becoming the norm, teaching children about responsible and respectful online behavior early on is essential. Not everyone is their friend; some may not have their best interest in mind!

Social skills form the foundation for building and maintaining positive relationships with family, peers, teachers, and other community members. Effective communication and cooperation contribute to better academic performance and a positive learning environment in the classroom. The long-term benefit of learning social skills will influence a child's ability to collaborate in the workplace, form romantic relationships, and navigate social situations throughout life. Social skills enable children to engage positively with their community, fostering a sense of citizenship and responsibility.

C are: Emotional skills encompass a range of abilities that enable kids to recognize, understand, manage, and express their own emotions, as well as empathize with the emotions of others. Children need to learn how to identify their feelings and those of others accurately. Teaching children to articulate their thoughts and emotions effectively helps them communicate their needs and build stronger relationships.

Younger children especially need to develop emotional regulation. Helping children appropriately manage their emotions, including anger and frustration, is essential for peaceful interactions. Learning to control impulses will allow them to follow multiple-step directions despite disruptions.

Starting off in their own bubble, children don't always think about how others feel. They tend to be impulsive. Learning to think before acting and making choices that consider the feelings of others will require plenty of practice. Communication skills like active listening, where a child pays attention to what the speaker is saying and responds appropriately, foster empathy and understanding. Empathy involves recognizing and understanding the emotions of others. Teach them to be bucket fillers, encouraging acts of kindness, showing gratitude and empathy. It promotes compassion and the ability to offer support.

Emotional skills help children bounce back from setbacks and adversity. They learn to persevere through challenges and setbacks. They understand that they have control over how they react to situations, which empowers children to take more responsibility for their actions and emotions.

These skills contribute to emotional well-being by helping children manage their emotions, develop self-confidence, and build a sense of belonging. Parents, caregivers, and educators play a crucial role in nurturing these skills in children to help them become emotionally intelligent, empathetic, resilient, and self-confident.

Strong: Physical skills encompass a wide range of motor and physical abilities that children develop during their early years of education. They will need to learn different types of movements and exercise various muscle groups. Gross motor includes large, whole-body movements like running, jumping, skipping, and crawling. Fine motor skills involve precise movements of the fingers and hands, such as writing, drawing, using scissors, or buttoning clothing. Physical abilities include coordination, balance, endurance, flexibility, speed, agility, and reaction time. All these skills are essential for developing muscular strength and will help with their overall physical well-being.

Practice gross motor skills by climbing a tree, doing jumping jacks, throwing, and catching. Tying shoelaces, using utensils, playing musical instruments, and coloring within the lines are all activities requiring fine motor skills. Gymnastics, dance, and yoga for kids are fun ways to work on flexibility. Skating and bike riding all need balance. Running and swimming will increase endurance. Ball skills such as basketball, volleyball, baseball, soccer, and tennis can help with coordination, speed, agility, and reaction time. Practicing several physical activities allows your child to explore their interests while developing strength.

The focus in elementary school should be having FUN while learning fundamental skills. An active lifestyle is not only important for physical health and development but also plays a significant role in a child's ability to engage in organized sports. Recreational activities with family and friends are also excellent opportunities for children to enhance their physical capabilities. Providing opportunities for skill development can contribute to a child's well-rounded development during their elementary school years.

The ABC'S are closely interrelated and intertwined in a child's development. These four domains influence and support one another, creating a complex web of interconnected abilities that shape a child's overall growth. Practicing fundamental skills at an early age gives your child a head start in life.

Chapter 3

1, 2, 3 - Method for Learning Skills

From the moment a child is born, we care for our babies for their survival. Although well-intentioned, this can easily transition into helicopter parenting, where we become overly controlling. We care so deeply that we want to ensure their safety and success. Let's face it: with busy schedules, we tend to feel constantly rushed, and some tasks are just easier and faster for a more experienced adult.

However, we are not helping our kids by micromanaging every aspect of their lives. Research shows that a balanced approach, which allows children to develop independence, resilience, and problem-solving skills, is more beneficial for their long-term well-being. Healthy parenting involves finding a balance between providing guidance, support, and structure while also allowing children the space and freedom to learn from their experiences and make their own choices. Encouraging autonomy, fostering resilience, and promoting open communication are more effective in helping children grow into confident and capable individuals.

Elementary kids are usually eager to learn new skills if we are patient in showing them how to be successful. Kids take pride in doing things for themselves. Build a foundation of life skills that will serve them for one day living on their own.

Teaching life skills takes 3 steps:

1 **Guidance:** Begin teaching life skills early, as soon as your child is capable of understanding and following basic instructions. This sets a foundation for more complex skills later on. Younger children love to have quality time with adults and seek their approval. Clearly communicate your expectations to your child. Let them know what you want them to learn, why it's essential, and how to accomplish a goal.

Children often learn by observing their parents. Demonstrate the life skills you want them to know through your actions and behaviors. Storytelling is also valuable when practicing skills. You can find videos online or books at your local library to lead by example. First watch, then do.

Incorporate life skills into daily routines and activities. For example, involve your child in cooking, cleaning, grocery shopping, and other household tasks. You can turn cooking into a creative culinary adventure or make a game out of having them tidy up their room. You wouldn't ask your five-year-old to make dinner on their own. Cooking is a learned skill. Simply telling your child to clean their room will leave them overwhelmed by the monumental mess they've made, and you'll find your child sitting amongst it, not knowing where to begin. Breaking down a task into easy-to-follow steps by showing them how to organize and find a home for their belongings will be more impactful, with each step giving them a feeling of success and boosting their confidence.

Ask them, "What happens when no one cleans?" Explain why it's essential to keep their room clean, such as being able to find a particular toy or preventing another person from injuring themselves accidentally by stepping and breaking their toys. Having a pet dog can indirectly motivate a child to keep their room clean. Things left on the floor can be chewed or, worse yet, used for marking territory. YUCK!

Make learning fun! See how fast they can accomplish a portion of the goal before a song ends and slowly work towards allowing them to do it independently. Try "The Clean Up" song by the Kiboomers. Don't take over doing a task or redoing it in front of them. They will realize that you will step in if they give up or do poorly. Unfortunately, the success of cleaning a room will depend on the want of your child. You'll still need to remind them to clean their room like a broken record, but one day, they will manage and maybe repeat the process with potential kids of their own.

2 **Support:** Practice, practice, practice! Teach them to divide more complex skills into smaller, manageable steps. This makes it easier for children to grasp and practice each part before moving on to the next. Ensure that the tools and equipment your child uses are appropriate for their age and size. This promotes safety and independence. Allow your child to take on appropriate responsibilities and make decisions. Encouraging independence fosters confidence and a sense of accomplishment.

Give your child choices whenever possible. For instance, let them choose what they want to wear, eat, or read. This helps them practice decision-making. By making good decisions, kids can create a path in life for themselves instead of being reactive to life that happens to them. Start small by giving your kids choices, building on that until they can think of the consequences (good or bad) of the decisions they might make. Your support will comfort them, giving them the confidence to try new things.

Offer praise and encouragement when your child successfully completes a life skill task. Positive reinforcement motivates them to continue learning. Leave Easter eggs in uplifting notes hidden in their lunch boxes or make a bookmark note in something they are reading. Offer constructive feedback when necessary. Discuss ways for improvement. Help your child learn from their mistakes. Celebrate your child's successes, no matter how small, and acknowledge their efforts and achievements to boost their self-esteem. Understand that children may not master a skill immediately. Be patient and available to answer questions, provide guidance, and offer emotional support as your child navigates new challenges and experiences.

3 Structure: Capitalize on teachable moments when they arise. To combat their gimmie stage while shopping, use the opportunity to discuss the concept of money, values, and needs vs. wants. Include your child in planning activities, such as meal planning or organizing a family outing. This teaches them how to make plans and set goals. Emphasize safety rules and precautions when teaching skills that involve potential risks, such as cooking or using tools.

Utilize online resources, educational materials, family, friends, and community members to supplement your teachings. There are many resources available that can make learning life skills more engaging. Consistently reinforce and practice life skills with your child. Repetition helps solidify their understanding and competence. Encourage your child to ask questions and express curiosity. Be open to their inquiries and provide explanations when needed.

Teach the what, why, and how of learning a skill. Remember that every child is unique, and their readiness to learn and master life skills may vary. Tailor your approach to your child's individual needs, interests, and abilities. Create a positive and supportive learning environment that fosters their independence and self-confidence.

Motivating elementary kids to learn life skills can be a rewarding but sometimes challenging task. Parents can use various strategies to encourage their children's interest and active participation in acquiring these valuable skills.

Here are some effective ways to motivate elementary-aged kids:

- **Make It Fun:** Incorporate games, hands-on activities, and interactive experiences into the learning process. When kids enjoy what they're doing, they are more likely to stay engaged and motivated.

- **Set Age-Appropriate Goals:** Break down the skills into manageable steps and set achievable goals. Celebrate small successes along the way to boost their confidence and motivation.
- **Provide Autonomy:** Take a step back and let them lead. Giving them some control makes them more invested in the process.
- **Use Positive Reinforcement:** Offer praise, encouragement, and rewards when they make efforts or demonstrate progress in learning life skills. Positive reinforcement can boost their motivation.
- **Be a Role Model:** Children often learn by observing their parents or caregivers. Model the behavior and skills you want them to know; they will likely follow suit.
- **Make It Relevant:** Explain the practical importance of the life skill. Show how it will benefit them in daily life, now and in the future. When kids understand the relevance, they are more motivated to learn.
- **Provide Choices:** Offer choices when possible. For example, if you're teaching healthy eating habits, let them select between a few healthy snack options. This gives them a sense of control.
- **Use Real-Life Scenarios:** Books are a great way to introduce concepts, but try incorporating real-life situations into the learning process. Discuss scenarios requiring the skill and ask how they would handle them.
- **Set Challenges:** Present challenges or problems that can be solved using the life skill you're teaching. Kids often enjoy overcoming obstacles and taking on new challenges.
- **Create a Learning Environment:** Keep resources, tools, and materials readily available to facilitate practice and exploration.
- **Collaborate:** Involve them in decision-making and planning. Let them help plan a reasonable gift budget or savings goals if you're teaching financial literacy.

- **Show Enthusiasm:** Demonstrate your enthusiasm and interest in teaching life skills. Your enthusiasm can be contagious and inspire them to be more motivated.
- **Peer Engagement:** Arrange opportunities for kids to learn with or from their peers. Group activities or projects can make learning more enjoyable and foster motivation.
- **Offer Responsibilities:** Gradually give them more responsibilities related to the skill. This can provide a sense of accomplishment and encourage further learning.
- **Connect to Interests:** Find ways to connect life skills to your child's interests and hobbies. If they love cooking, focus on kitchen and meal preparation skills.
- **Feedback and Reflection:** Encourage them to reflect on their progress and discuss what they've learned. Provide constructive feedback and suggestions for improvement.
- **Variety and Exploration:** Introduce various life skills and let them explore different areas of interest. This can help them discover what they're passionate about.
- **Be Patient:** Understand that motivation may ebb and flow. Be patient and supportive during times when they may be less interested in learning a particular skill.
- **Celebrate Achievements:** Celebrate milestones and achievements related to life skills. Recognize their efforts and hard work, even for small accomplishments.
- **Keep It Positive:** Maintain a positive and encouraging attitude throughout the learning process. Avoid criticism or negativity, as it can demotivate children.

Remember, your voice becomes your child's inner voice. As a parent, your words carry a profound impact on your child's development. The way you communicate and the words you choose become your child's inner voice, shaping their self-perception and guiding their decision-making throughout life.

As parents, we should avoid being overly critical and focus less on what our children do wrong and put more praise on what they do right. Let your child know that it's okay to make mistakes. Your child will make mistakes, and those moments should be learning opportunities rather than grounds for a negative self-image. Try to be cognitive that what you say to your children will ultimately be what they believe of themselves. Positive and affirming words from a parent can instill confidence, resilience, and a sense of worth in a child. Conversely, harsh or critical language may create self-doubt and insecurity.

Parenting can be stressful, and in those times, before saying something negative out of anger or frustration, ask yourself if what you are about to say is how you want your child to value themselves. For instance, saying something like "You are so clumsy" or "Don't be stupid" labels your child that they are clumsy or stupid! A parent's words serve as a powerful mirror, reflecting how a child sees themselves and the world around them. Therefore, the words parents use play a pivotal role in nurturing a child's self-esteem, emotional well-being, and overall outlook on life.

Help create a positive and nurturing environment that fosters a love for learning and the development of essential life skills. Motivation can vary from child to child, and what works for one may not work for another. Be flexible and open to adapting your approach based on your child's unique interests and needs.

Chapter 4

Milestones

Milestones for elementary-age children, typically ranging from ages 5 to 11, can vary widely depending on individual development and factors such as environment and opportunities. However, there are general developmental milestones that can serve as a rough guide for parents and caregivers. Here are some milestones by year:

Kindergarten, Age 5-6:

Cognitive Development:

- Recognizes and recites the alphabet.
- Can write their name.
- Begins to read simple words and sentences.
- Can explain objects and their uses.
- Is able to repeat information.
- Counts to 100 and may start basic addition and subtraction.
- Knows their phone number.
- Is familiar with the days of the week.
- Can follow a sequence of three or more steps.

- Talks frequently.
- Curious about the world around them.
- Eager to please others and make them happy.
- Working on good manners.
- Uses their imagination more.
- Enjoys arts and crafts, staying busy.
- Practices skills to become better.
- Likes to mimic adults.

Social and Emotional Development:

- May show increasing independence and a sense of self-identity.
- Develops empathy and understanding of others' feelings. Learning how to resolve conflicts.
- Enjoys playing with peers and forming friendships. Prefers playing with kids the same gender.
- Becomes more self-aware and self-regulating emotionally.

Physical Development:

- Gains better control over fine motor skills, such as drawing, writing, and using scissors. Can differentiate right and left hands. Dresses themselves and knows how to tie their shoes.
- Enjoys helping in the kitchen. Have your child involved in preparing meals so they grow up with healthy eating habits.
- May like learning to play sports. However, organized sports may be frustrating and may discourage future participation. Focus on fun and learning fundamentals to boost confidence.
- Can ride a bike and maybe roller skate.
- Shows improved coordination and balance in physical activities. Can walk backwards and balance on one foot for several seconds.
- Starts to lose their baby teeth and permanent teeth begin to come in.

- Growing 2-2.5" on average per year, around 4-7 lbs per year.
- Kids should have at least 1 hour of physical activity per day. The more, the better to keep them active and ready for a good night's sleep.
- Sleeps 9-12 hours a night. Consistent bedtime, especially for school nights.

First Grade, Ages 6-7:

Cognitive Development:

- Reads and comprehends simple books.
- Develops a better understanding of mathematical operations.
- Knows their address.
- Knows the months of the year.
- Begins to develop problem-solving skills.

Social and Emotional Development:

- More aware of how others perceive them.
- May become more aware of gender roles and differences. Starting to make comparisons.
- May show more signs of jealousy of others and siblings.

Physical Development:

- Can groom themselves.
- Fine motor skills continue to improve, allowing for more detailed artwork and writing.
- Best in non-competitive league sports. Not sure what interests them without more exposure.

Second Grade, Ages 7-8:

Cognitive Development:

- Reads more fluently and enjoys a variety of books and genres.
- Understands basic mathematical concepts, like time and money.
- Explores creative and imaginative thinking.
- Enjoys collecting things.
- Social and Emotional Development:
- Forms stronger friendships and may develop close bonds with peers.
- Shows increasing empathy and understanding of others' perspectives.
- May become more self-conscious about appearance and social status.

Physical Development:

- Fine motor skills continue to improve, allowing for intricate drawing and writing.
- Starting to use tools like a hammer and screwdriver.
- Gross motor skills develop further, enhancing athletic abilities and coordination: skips, chases, throws, and catches. May not be interested in competitive sports but willing to be active.

Third Grade, Ages 8-9: Tween years, 8-12!

Cognitive Development:

- Reading skills become more advanced, with a greater focus on comprehension and critical thinking. Reading more and may actually enjoy it!
- Can name months and days of the week.

- Math skills progress to include more complex operations and problem-solving. Can count backwards and multiples.
- Shows an interest in exploring various academic subjects.

Social and Emotional Development:

- Develops a sense of responsibility and may take on more responsibilities at home.
- Enjoys group activities.
- Begins to understand more complex social dynamics and friendships.
- Interested in broadening friendships with the opposite gender. Curious about relationships with them but not in an open manner.
- Shows increased empathy and concern for others.

Physical Development:

- Fine motor skills allow for more detailed artwork and writing. Understands the concept of space.
- Gross motor skills continue to develop, contributing to improved athletic abilities. Becoming more competitive.
- Puberty in girls can start showing signs (range from 8-13 years old). May be more emotional due to hormonal changes and begins showing signs of physical changes. May become more aware of body images.

Fourth Grade, Ages 9-10:

Cognitive Development:

- Reading skills reach a more advanced level, with the ability to comprehend complex texts.
- More sophisticated ability to complete thoughts or feelings.
- Math skills become more sophisticated, including concepts like fractions and decimals.
- Shows an interest in more in-depth and specialized subjects.

- Maybe be more tired, moody, or change interests day-to-day.
- More aware of dangers which can cause anxiety.
- Longer attention spans.
- Can complete Lego instructions on their own.
- Playing games or puzzles requiring spatial awareness.

Social and Emotional Development:

- Demonstrates greater independence and self-sufficiency.
- Forms close friendships and may experience peer pressure.
- Strong desire to belong to a group and establish their place within the social order of their school.
- Begins to think about future goals and plans.
- May experience their first romantic feelings but will keep it to themselves.

Physical Development:

- Fine motor skills are well-developed, allowing for advanced artistic endeavors. Can draw from different perspectives. May enjoy sewing.
- Gross motor skills continue to improve, contributing to sports and physical activities. May enjoy competitive sports.

Fifth Grade, Age 10-11:

Cognitive Development:

- Can write stories well. May enjoy writing letters or emails.
- Reads for enjoyment and interests.

Social and Emotional Development:

- Enjoys hanging out with friends. Will want to meet up, talk, or text.
- Likes and respects parents.

Physical Development:

- Puberty in boys can start around this age. Voice may change, as well as other physical changes.
- Growth spurts are common.
- They will show improved endurance and coordination.

***Puberty is a period of significant physical, emotional, and social changes that typically occur during the adolescent years. The onset and progression of puberty can vary widely among individuals, and some children may not experience noticeable changes until later in their teenage years. For those who do enter puberty earlier, it's crucial for parents and caregivers to provide guidance, support, and reassurance during this oftentimes challenging phase of development. Maintaining open lines of communication, ensuring access to accurate information, and fostering a positive self-image are all essential aspects of helping elementary-aged kids navigate the effects of puberty. The early changes that can affect elementary-aged kids are cognitive, social, emotional, and physical.

Puberty signs to take note of:

Cognitive Changes:

- Risky Behavior: During puberty, you may see changes in reasoning abilities and
- decision-making that can lead to risk-taking behaviors.
- Focus: Puberty can sometimes impact a child's concentration.
- Q&A: They may be curious about physical and sexual development. Parents should be prepared for these discussions and maintain open, honest, and age-appropriate communication. You may be proactive and consider bringing up topics before they ask.

Social Changes:

- Friendships: Puberty can influence friendships as children may start forming closer bonds with some peers while distancing themselves from others.
- Peer Pressure: Social pressures related to appearance, clothing, and behavior may become more prominent during this time.
- Interest in Romantic Relationships: Some children may begin to show interest in romantic relationships, which can affect their interactions with peers.

Emotional Changes:

- Mood Swings: Hormonal changes during puberty can lead to mood swings, making some children more irritable or emotional at times.
- Self-Esteem: Changes in physical appearance may impact self-esteem, leading to increased self-consciousness or body image concerns.

Physical Changes:

- Growth Spurts: Some children may experience growth spurts, leading to an increase in height and weight. Girls and boys may see physical changes that may make them or their peers self-conscious. Body image and eating problems can be an issue, even this young.
- Body Hair: Boys may start to develop facial hair, while both boys and girls may notice the growth of pubic and underarm hair.
- Body Odor: As sweat glands become more active, children may develop body odor, necessitating the use of deodorant.

A helpful resource online is amaze.org/jr/. There, you will find videos to help parents explain what can be uncomfortable sexual education topics. Set up a My Amaze account to share specific videos with your children on a protected page. Amaze, jr is geared towards kids 4-9 years of age. You can find additional resources for older children at amaze.org.

It's important to remember that developmental milestones can vary among children, and not all children will reach these milestones at the same time or in the same way. Additionally, these milestones are general guidelines and may not apply to every child. If you have concerns about your child's development, it's advisable to consult with a healthcare professional or educator for guidance and assessment.

Chapter 5

Kindergarten

Woo-hoo, you are no longer paying for preschool! If your child didn't go to preschool, this may be the first time your child is away from their family and the familiarity of what they know. They will be around kids their own age and learning to take direction from new adult figures. This will be a time of building the foundations of social skills and seeing firsthand how they progress without holding your hand.

Kids at this age have a plethora of natural skills that should not be discouraged but managed. They are curious, wanting to absorb information. Kids have a great imagination that shows when they play. Their creativity is less constrained by rules and boundaries, allowing for more imaginative expressions. Channel their energy in positive ways and enable kids to be kids. Foster their innate skills.

When most kids turn five years old, you can start to incorporate daily chores for 15-20 minutes to practice several useful life skills. Consider a potential reward system. Stickers only work for so long. Try using pretend money that your child can exchange for screen time or working towards a short-term goal. That could eventually grow into an allowance and tie in with financial literacy.

You can teach many of these life skills in tandem. Your child can learn several skills through the following activities. Here are some ideas on teaching appropriate life skills to kindergartners, along with their benefits and activities to implement these skills:

Communication Skills:

Benefits: Enhances verbal and non-verbal communication skills.

Activities:

- Storytelling: Read, read, read! Set the foundation for a love of reading by reading to your child daily. Encourage your child to tell stories from picture books, their imagination, or draw pictures to express themselves. Provide kids with story starters or sentence prompts, and have them complete the stories or sentences. This fosters creativity and verbal expression.
- Facetime: Call your relatives; grandparents love to hear from their grandkids, and have your kids practice asking questions and talking about things that matter to them. Talk about school activities, time spent with family and friends, or things they are looking forward to doing. They should practice active listening, showing interest, and waiting for their turn to speak without rudely interrupting.
- Rose, Bud, and Thorn: As your kids are away at school most of the weekdays, it's only natural that parents want to know about their day. Asking your child, "How was your day?" will often result in lackluster answers, if any. I didn't come up with this, but we use this as a mindful and easy way for our kids to share. "What was your rose, bud, and thorn?" is more of a leading question that helps generate answers. The rose should reflect something good that happened, the bud is something they are looking forward to, and the thorn is a negative experience. Oftentimes, we have thought-provoking answers and further discussions, that enable open communication. Highlight the positives and work through the disappointments or challenges with your child.

- Show and Tell: Practice at home in a comfortable environment. Allow them to talk about their favorite toys. Work on eye contact and speaking to an audience of family members.
- Neighborhood walk: Encourage your child to ask questions. If you don't know the answers, teach your child how to use verbal prompts on a device to find the answers. Discuss how to be gentle with babies, plants, and pets (any living things). Discuss different non-verbal cues they can show. Use teachable moments on how to approach a dog. Have your child ask an owner if they can pet a dog. Show them how to introduce their hand and allow the dog to sniff it before petting.
- Sing: Have your kids memorize a song and recite it. You could start with nursery rhymes and holiday songs. Once they can read, the Amazon Echo Show is great for learning the words to more complex songs. When your child can read more fluently, karaoke can also be helpful in learning other languages!
- Conversation Cards: Similar to playing cards, each card has a topic for discussion, which can be used during car rides or at the family dinner table. They can be purchased online or made by your family members. You could have anonymous questions or topics placed in a large container, and each member can fish out a card. Everyone should participate in answering the questions or topic.
- Telephone Game: Practice active listening and memorization. One person whispers a message that needs to be whispered to the next person. This goes on until the last person receives and recites the message. The message usually gets messed up along the way, but it's funny for kids to hear the difference from start to finish. Of course, they enjoy whispering confused messages.
- Tongue Twisters: Try repeating, "Susy sells seashells by the seashore," and the likes quickly and accurately for several iterations. This can improve clarity in speech.

Creative Skills:

Benefits: A little boredom can bring out the best imagination. Nurture creative thinking and problem-solving abilities to encourage innovation and adaptability.

Activities:

- Artspace: Parents can create a space for building, drawings, and writing.
- Mini theater stage: Put on plays with puppets or costumes.

Decision-making Skills:

Benefits: Encourages independence and self-sufficiency. Learn how to plan and when to ask for help.

Activities:

- Plan an activity with your family: Decide what to do, how to get there, and what to bring. Help them plan a picnic, a day at the beach, or attend a community event.
- Pack an overnight bag: Next time your kids stay overnight at their grandparents' house, have them help pack their own bag with your guidance.
- Busy airport: By the age of 5, kids are able to fly direct domestic flights alone as unaccompanied minors (age 8 for connecting flights). WOW! If you are a frequent traveler, try teaching your child how to get around an airport, reading departure and arrival screens when they can read. When you are comfortable allowing your kids to fly without you, request a "gate pass" from the airline to accompany your child through security to the departure gate and ask for electronic ticketing so there's no need to worry about losing physical tickets. You'll also want to make sure not to book the last flight of the day! Most airlines are good about having an attendant watch over your child, but I have heard stories suggesting this is not always the case.

- Shopping: Play store at home, set up a shop with items around the house, and practice the very basic concepts of how money is used. Then, consider what you have at home and go to an actual store to buy ingredients needed for a recipe or shop for a project. Check pricing, quality, and quantity of items and help decide what to buy.
- Homework: Even if their school teacher doesn't require homework, you'll still want to practice sight words, reading, and math concepts. This is an excellent time to work on patience. It's a skill that even adults struggle with, and kids can benefit from delayed gratification. Teaching kids that they need to do their homework before going out to play will set the groundwork for self-regulation early on. It only gets busier from here on out with more homework, sports, and club activities. Have your child think about the consequences of not doing their homework and reward them when they get their homework done. Praise your child for working hard on things they struggle with and spend some extra time playing a game with them as a reward.

Emotional Regulation:

Benefits: Encourages self-awareness and emotional resilience.

Activities:

- Feelings Charades: Play a game of charades where your child acts out different emotions or has to guess the emotion you are acting out.
- Emotion Cards: Use cards with faces displaying various emotions and discuss what makes them feel those emotions.
- Reading Books: Stop to discuss how a character feels in different situations and why.
- Practice Bucket-filling: A term referring to positive action and behavior. The concept of being a bucket filler is based on the idea that each person has an invisible bucket that represents their emotional well-being and happiness. When we do or say kind and positive things, we are "filling"

someone else's bucket, which makes them feel good and happy. Promote a caring and supportive community where we uplift and support one another by being bucket-fillers, not bucket-dippers.

Hygiene:

Benefits: Promotes good health, cleanliness, and self-care. Contributes to feeling good about oneself. Good hygiene routines set healthy habits that they can use for the rest of their lives.

Activities:

- Create a daily hygiene routine: Have your child think of hygiene tasks they must complete throughout a typical day. Create a picture/word checklist for them to go through. If you have a smart home device, your child can learn how to use prompts that help them set up task alarms.
- Hand-washing Song: One of the good things to come from Covid was the ability for my kids to perfect their hand-washing skills. They were taught to sing the Happy Birthday song twice while scrubbing the front and back of their hands, as well as in between their fingers and focusing on their fingertips. Songs can create a fun and memorable way for your child to make the learning process enjoyable. Sing together while washing hands after they use the bathroom, when returning home from a day out, before they eat, and more often when they are sick.
- Teeth Brushing App: Download an app to monitor and track daily teeth brushing, making it a fun and rewarding routine. Colgate has a base that attaches to their toothbrushes and works with their app, Magik and hum. It shows kids where they should be brushing and makes a game out of it. There's a parent side where you can set up notifications and monitor their activities. Have them brush in a circular motion to prevent their gums from receding in the future. You'll also want to ensure they are flossing by

doing it together. Unfortunately, I haven't found an app for that yet!

- Dressing Dolls and Themselves: Have kids practice dressing their dolls. Give them a variety of outfits to choose from - casual, fancy, sporty, etc. Have them practice using zippers, snaps, and buttons. They can also practice hair grooming, ponytails, and braiding skills on their dolls. Just before the start of the school year, let your kids have a say in the clothes they wear by bringing them along for back-to-school shopping. This was always a tradition in my house. Show them how to use a belt and practice using the buttons in adjustable waists. Encourage them to lay out their outfits the night before school.
- Tying Shoes: If they haven't learned yet, check online for resources to help you teach your child to tie their shoes. They can also learn to lace their shoes. Take out the laces and start the thread with beads of their initials or fun shapes. Have them continue lacing the rest of the shoe and end with tying them.
- Role-play: Practice going to the doctor or dental office. Let the child take on roles such as a doctor, dentist, or chef and act out hygiene routines associated with those professions. Talk about the consequences of not practicing good hygiene, but be sure also to discuss why we have regular check-ups and teeth cleanings. Pretend you are sick and have your child correct you on how to blow your nose, sneeze in your elbow, and cover up a cough.
- Simon Says. A fun way for kids to practice listening and following directions like, "Simon says, wash your hands." "Brush your teeth." Your child should act out all the activities that start with Simon Says and is out if you don't say Simon Says. Switch roles so they give you the commands.
- Germ Tag: Your child pretends to be a germ trying to infect others, and the goal is to avoid getting tagged. Once tagged, that person is also a germ, helping to infect others until

everyone has been tagged. The last person tagged starts a
new game.

- Reading: Go to your local library to find books regarding
  proper hygiene. Look for colorful illustrations and engaging
  stories. Read to your child, and when they can, have them
  read to you. Ask your child hypothetical questions like,
  'What would you do in this situation?' or, specifically, 'Why
  don't we share things worn on our heads?" LICE! Be
  proactive in teaching your kids healthy habits.

Kitchen Skills:

Benefits: Promotes self-sufficiency and safety in the kitchen.

Activities:

- Cookie Decorating: Let your child help bake cookies. They
  can help measure and mix the ingredients, keep track of the
  timer, and decorate with simple toppings like icing and
  sprinkles.
- Fruit and Veggie Prep: Take your child grocery shopping
  and show them how to choose fruits and veggies. Involve
  them in washing and cutting fruits and vegetables with
  supervision. Have them peel bananas and oranges.
- Food art: Sort fruits and veggies by color and have them
  create a rainbow platter. Or use them to make faces and
  other pictures or to embellish a meal.
- Make lunch for the family: Help them prepare and make
  simple sandwiches. Have them plan what kind of
  sandwich they want to make. What will they need for a
  peanut butter and jelly, deli or vegetarian sandwich? Help
  them prepare things like a plate, dull knife, condiments,
  and other ingredients. Teach them how to spread
  condiments (and butter) onto bread. Have them choose a
  healthy, non-cooked side dish. You could prepare some
  fresh lemonade together. Practice setting the table and
  carefully bring items from the kitchen to the table. Be sure
  to tell your child how lovely the presentation is and how

delicious everything tastes. They will be brimming with pride.

- School snacks: Have various options available, at their eye level, in the fridge and pantry. Allow them to be responsible for choosing their own snacks. Have them explore the uses of various bags and containers for storing their snacks. You will want to remind them during their morning routine to put their snacks in their backpacks.
- Guessing game: Explain the use of kitchen appliances. Take turns naming appliances and finding their locations. Describe a use and have your child point to the right appliance or name it.
- Food Storage: Have your child play around with different ways to store food in containers and bags. Make sure they know how to open and close them properly. Show them when and how to use plastic wrap and aluminum foil. Practice folding down bags and using clips to prevent snacks from going stale.
- Opening Snacks and Cartons: They should be getting a lot of practice in school. Show them how to open their milk cartons without digging their fingers inside. Have them peel the carton seal and use pressure on the sides to pry it open. Fruit snacks are tricky, even for adults, but have them slowly peel back the foil or plastic without applying too much pressure to the container. Chances are there will be some spills, so provide a napkin for them to clean themselves and any spills.

Mindfulness:

Benefits: Conscious living helps kids manage emotions, showing gratitude and resourcefulness. They also learn to conserve resources and reduce waste. By showing your child how to appreciate the interconnectedness of all life forms and the impact of human actions on the environment, they learn to have empathy and compassion for all living things.

Activities:

- Gratitude Journal: Have your child draw or write things they are thankful for each day, week, or once a month.
- Environmental Superhero: Teach them the concept of reduce, reuse, and recycle. How can they conserve energy and water? Teach them to turn off the lights they are not using. Set a time limit for showers. How are they reducing waste? How much toilet paper should they use? (This might also help you with your clogged toilets.) Show them how they can donate or sell their unused items. If they make some money, take them to a thrift store to find a reward. In your house or neighborhood, play a recycling game where they find paper, plastic, and cans to put in the recycling bin.
- Breathing Buddies: Have your child lie down with a stuffed animal on their belly. Inhale deeply, making the stuffed animal rise, and exhale slowly, making it fall. This helps children become aware of their breath, releasing any stress and helping them relax. Try using breathing exercises when your child needs help with regulating their emotions.
- Nature walks: Spending time in nature has been linked to improved mental and emotional well-being. Take your child on a nature walk, whether in a park, garden, or even your backyard. Encourage them to use their senses to explore nature, such as feeling the texture of leaves, smelling flowers, or listening to bird songs. Discuss the different sensations and how they can bring awareness to the present moment.
- If you visit US National Parks, stop by a Visitor's Center and ask for the Junior Ranger program. Participation is from ages 5-13, but with help, younger kids can complete activities. There are age-grouped activities coded in the booklets. Usually, there is a section where your child will be asked to sit and mindfully absorb their surroundings. The entire booklet is filled with opportunities for your child to be present and aware of their time there. The program is a memorable way for children to actively enjoy our National Parks. Have them turn in their completed booklet to a Park Ranger, where they will state an oath to protect nature and

receive a badge. We like to use the provided stamps on the back of the badges to remember when we visited. We purchased ranger vests for our kids to pin their collected badges. Kids love to collect things!

Money Awareness:

Benefits: Practices critical thinking and problem-solving. Children learn to analyze choices, consider consequences, and make informed decisions.

Activities:

- Role-play: Set up a store or restaurant. Make purchases until the money runs out, and then take turns. They will simply like the process of paying and receiving change. The correct amount isn't important at this age.
- Coin Rubbings: Make coin rubbings by placing coins under a piece of paper and gently rubbing a crayon or pencil over them. This helps them become familiar with different coin designs.
- Guessing game: You can try to introduce the value of coins and bills. Show them the similarities and differences of each. Have them try to match the correct values.
- Allowance: Simple chores can be compensated with play or real money. Chores help teach the connection between work and earning money. Have them think of a goal to work towards, such as a toy or special outing. Have them use a piggy bank to store their money and discuss how they will need to save for their goal. Delayed gratification teaches them to save and wait for something they want rather than spending impulsively. They can cash it in when they earn enough. You could fine them for bad behavior! Children learn to be accountable for their financial choices and must care for their money.
- Tooth Fairy: They will be starting to lose their baby teeth. If they receive glitter-sprinkled money from the fairy, remind them of the option to save it in their piggy bank.

- Shopping: For the next birthday party they are invited to or a gift-giving holiday, take them to the store. Have them store and carry money securely in a wallet or enclosed area of a purse or bag. Set a monetary limit and have them choose an appropriate gift. Talk to them about the difference in needs vs. wants. Take the time to teach them how to make informed decisions when purchasing goods (and services). Have them compare similar items and consider quality and quantity. Help them think of what the receiver wants, not what they want. Teach them to be a thoughtful gift giver.
- Reading: Giving does not come naturally for some people. Reading stories may help them better understand and encourage children to set aside a portion of their money for charitable donations. Discuss the importance of giving to those in need. Have them help choose items for a local food drive. If you are a part of a church, you could teach the importance of tithing. This will help them be responsible and show empathy.

Problem-Solving:

Benefits: Develops critical thinking and decision-making skills.

Activities:

- Puzzle Time: Work on age-appropriate puzzles together to encourage problem-solving. You cut up a poster or photo and have your child put the pieces back together.
- Building Challenges: Use building sets to create challenges that require creative solutions. Duplos and Mega Bloks are larger, chunkier versions of Legos and more manageable for little hands. Simple wooden blocks often come in forms to build a small pretend community. Magna-tiles connect tiles with magnets. They also have a racetrack version. There are plenty of other plastic building tracks, and some are even glow-in-the-dark.

- Walk in the Rain: Have your child decide how to dress and what to bring. This also applies to playing in the snow. Help guide them, but let them try to work out how to prepare.

Safety Skills:

Benefits: Teaches awareness and safety in various situations.

Activities:

- Crossing the Street Game: Use a pretend road and toy cars to teach safe traffic safety skills. Street-crossing skills are beneficial while biking around the neighborhood, walking to school, or playing outside. Think of things like stop, look, and listen before crossing the street. Their instinct will be to run after their ball if it goes in the street, but why is that not a good idea? Have them obey traffic signals and use crosswalks.
- Biking: Teach your child how to ride a bike and make sure they wear their helmet (also for skating, skateboarding, skiing, snowboarding, etc). Start off by using a balance bike or training wheels. Once you feel your child knows how to balance, take off the training wheels. There are excellent videos online to teach you and your child how to ride safely and how to take the training wheels off for good. Learning to ride a bike is a memorable childhood milestone for both of you! Once your child is more comfortable riding their bikes, practice using proper hand signals for turning left, right, and stopping. They'll have to be able to steer using one hand while signaling to those behind them. Take your child for longer rides in the community.
- Water Safety: Your child will be in a bathtub, near a pool, or at the beach. Water safety skills are essential, and so is your undivided attention to your child. No one thinks drowning will happen to them, but it can be fast and silent. It can happen to your child or you. Globally, the highest drowning rates are among children 1–4 years, followed by children 5–9 years, according to stopdrowningnow.org. Your child

needs to learn how to float, tread water, and ideally how to swim from a young age. Have your child take lessons at the local YMCA or see if your local pool offers them. Teach them how surfaces with water are especially slippery and that it's easy to fall and be injured. Have them walk near a pool and not run. Kids should know the potential risks of being pulled down by someone who is drowning and how to ask for help. They should also be taught about potential ocean risks, such as not turning their back to the ocean while building sandcastles on the beach, how waves come in intervals, and about rip currents. Be proactive with safety.

- Building at Home Depot or Lowes: You can find FREE build-it-yourself workshops where your child can practice using tools. Usually, on the first Saturday of each month, there is a building activity. You can find events online or call your local store to sign up in advance and to see what the upcoming projects will be. You will receive an apron, project kit, and certificate/pin upon completion. You will need to work with your child on the project, but eventually, they will learn to do more independently with practice. In addition to learning how to use tools safely, they can practice following directions and work towards accomplishing a short-term goal. It's a rewarding project that they can share, display, and play with at home.

- Safety Drill: Don't wait for an emergency. Have a plan. Practice a fire drill at home, teaching them how to stay low and exit safely. Demonstrate stop-drop-roll and practice together. Show how to use a variety of doors and locks in order to escape in an emergency. Teach them to be mindful, especially with their tiny fingers and hands, when opening and closing doors quickly. Practice using a garage opener and unlocking all the doors, including the car. If they need to in an emergency, tell them to break a window by throwing a hard object or kicking it and keep trying to find a way out. You will also want to make sure your child knows how to engage and disengage their own seatbelt. Ensure your kids know what to do in an emergency, if they are separated from you during a power outage or natural disaster, and where to meet.

- Basic First Aid Role Play: What should they do if they are injured? Teach them how to clean their skin, apply ointment or a bandaid, when and how to use heat or ice packs, and to know they can always ask an adult for help, especially if an injury is beyond their capacity. Discuss medication and vitamin safety.

- Emergency calls: This is another one you hope your child never has to use, but it is better to know before an emergency happens. Practice memorizing their full name, the names of both parents, how to describe their parents, their address, and phone number. Show your child how to use a phone that is accessible to them. Many of us no longer use landlines, so it's essential to show them how to use a cell phone in case of an emergency. The emergency call function to 911 is enabled unlocking your phone. However, you may consider unlocking your phone to practice how to search for family or neighbor contacts or how to press phone numbers manually to call 911 or poison control. Make a list of important phone numbers and place it on the fridge or another visible location. Role-play so your child knows how to answer potential questions like their name, contact information, and to describe scenarios for calling.

- Stranger Danger role-play: Try to approach the stranger danger topic in a way that empowers your child with knowledge while also avoiding unnecessary fear or anxiety. Emphasize safety rather than fear. Explain that a stranger is someone they haven't met before. Most people are kind and helpful, but they should not let strangers touch them, give them gifts, or ask them to go anywhere without your permission. Teach your child that if they are ever in a situation where they feel unsafe or uncomfortable, they should run to a trusted adult, such as a police officer, security guard, or a parent with children. Have them practice trusting their instincts. Teach them how to say "No!" firmly and loudly if a stranger approaches them.

Encourage your child to talk openly with you about their experiences and any concerns they may have related to strangers. Create a safe environment for them to share their feelings. Act out different scenarios with your child to help them practice responding in various situations. Regularly revisit the stranger danger rules and have conversations to reinforce the concepts. It's important to keep the information fresh in their minds.

- No-no square chant: Teach your child what is not appropriate touches, to set boundaries, and how to tell an adult if something were to happen. They should never be made to feel guilty or threatened by anyone, not a child or an adult. I learned this chant from my nieces, and it's valuable for all kids to learn. Have your child mimic your gestures.

- STOP! (Place your arm in front of you, palm facing out, fingertips facing up to signify stop.) Don't touch me there! (Use only your pointer finger to wag, move rapidly to and fro, the no signal back and forth.) That is my no-no square! (Use your hands to draw out an invisible square across your torso.)

- Lost: This is also an excellent time to discuss what to do if they get lost in a public space. Practice awareness of environmental clues and landmarks. Tell them it's best to stay visible in the last place they saw you or get help from a trusted adult like a police officer or mother with children. Prior to attending a large event like a fair, you can pre-purchase paper bracelets that are difficult for them to remove and write your phone number on the inside before sealing it around your child's wrist or ankle. Show your child and have them provide that information to a trusted adult if they are lost. They may have memorized your phone number but forget when they are in a stressful situation. Take a picture of them before going so that you have a recent image to share what they were wearing and how they looked in case they decide to play hide-and-seek, and can't be found! It's a scary situation to be in and it is best to be prepared.

Social Skills:

Benefits: Fosters positive relationships, empathy, and cooperation.

Activities:

- Dolls: Act out social scenarios with stuffed animals and dolls, teaching how to make new friends. Use polite greetings such as please, thank you, and excuse me. Express thoughts, manage emotions, listen, take turns, and share. Playing with a variety of toys is a good opportunity to show your kids how to embrace diversity and how to interact with those who may be different from them. Disney dolls can be used to teach your child different cultures and customs. You could expand on this by celebrating holidays from other parts of the world or look for events highlighting cultural traditions.
- Role-play: Similar to the use of dolls, pretend you and your child are at the doctor's office, grocery store, or restaurant. This is a chance for them to comfortably interact with you before practicing in the real world. At the imaginary restaurant, have them work on their table manners, like how to use a napkin and chew with their mouths closed properly. Show them how to draw someone's attention without interrupting rudely. Practice decision-making skills while choosing what to eat off a menu or how to serve guests.
- Playdates: Arrange playdates to practice taking turns and playing cooperatively with peers. Get to know the kids in their class and expand from there. They may find something to do on their own, but have some easy activities prepared just in case. Start off with an hour or two so that it's long enough to have fun but not overly drawn out.
- Sleepover: If they haven't yet, consider planning a time for your child to sleep over at their grandparents or with a cousin. Allow your child to spend the night away but in a

familiar environment. It's best to be prepared for a late-night pickup call, and that's okay. Encourage your child to stick it through, and if all else fails, try another night. Some kids love their independence, while others need a bit more comforting. They'll get there eventually.

- Boy Scouts and Girl Scouts: Join a scouting club that teaches life skills! Membership starts at the age of 5 and is ongoing. It's very affordable to join, but fees fluctuate depending on the troop. You can sign up online, and if you need additional help, there are member coordinators who can assist in finding a troop that suits your child. Meetings are a few times a month, depending on your troop. Your child will work on goals to earn badges. Character development is a large part of the programs where they instill values and help guide your child in making ethical decisions. Boy Scouts is also available for girls. Scouting clubs offer a holistic approach to child development, fostering intellectual, physical, social, and moral growth.

Tidying Up:

Benefits: Instills responsibility and organization skills.

Activities:

- Toy Sorting: Teach them to sort toys into bins based on type, color, or activity such as crafts, dress-up, or building.
- Clean-Up Race: Set a timer and challenge your child to clean up their mess as quickly as possible. Whether it be from spilling during a meal or an afternoon of playing with toys, have them be responsible for cleaning up. When they are a part of the clean-up process, they learn to be more careful and responsible, if ever so slightly.
- Little Helper: Small kids love to help wherever they can, especially if there is quality time with someone involved. What a great time to introduce supervised chores. Chores are actually fun for them!

- Have them practice place setting before a meal. Start with a picture or label printed placemats showing placeholders for proper cutlery, drinks, plates, bowls, and napkins. Have them clear the table and then dry dishes that you hand washed. Pull out a broom for them to sweep or vacuum where they ate their last meal.
- The laundry is a game in and of itself. You child can shoot their dirty clothes into the hamper like basketballs, and clothes from the dryer are like a sorting game or fun matching socks challenge. Learning to fold and put away clean clothes won't be as fun, but showing them how to use a hanger for clothes correctly adds a bit to the mix.
- Gardening? Buy them some cheap kid gloves, and the weeds will haphazardly disappear. They'll also be excited when you ask them to water the plants with the watering can. Have them choose which plants are ready to be harvested.
- Chances are they will go grocery shopping with you and would be happy to bring in the lighter groceries. They'd love to dust in easy-to-reach places and clean mirrors. At this age, you may not even have to ask for help. They are probably standing by, waiting to offer their assistance. Show them what needs to be done, work side-by-side, and don't be overly critical of how they accomplish a task.

Technology:

Benefits: Early exposure helps children adapt to our digital world. Technology is a strong motivator for learning. Use it to help find interests. Cognitive development is stimulated by promoting problem-solving, critical thinking, and memory skills.

Activities:

- Educational Games: Learning can be fun and interactive. Some apps and websites reinforce early learning concepts, including math, language, and literacy. Make sure your kids understand that they have to ask for permission or help before downloading something or clicking on a pop-up.

There may be some trial and error involved. You'll also need to manage how and when they are able to use digital devices.

- Access to Information: The internet provides a vast resource for information and knowledge. Teaching kids how to find and evaluate information online is a valuable skill. Some kid-safe web browsers and search engines filter content to ensure access to age-appropriate websites and information. This should still be closely monitored!
- E-books: Digital books have interactive features like read-aloud narration, animations, and touch-based interactions. These can help develop literacy skills while enjoying stories.
- Smart Toys: Interactive toys incorporate technology to engage children in learning through play. Examples include programmable robots, electronic building kits, and talking dolls.
- Digital Cameras: Allow them to take pictures and document their experiences. This fosters creativity and encourages observation skills. It's really interesting to see what catches their eye and see things from their perspective. Let them document a visit to the farmer's market or watch a sibling at their performance.
- Virtual Reality (VR) and Augmented Reality (AR): Some educational apps and experiences use VR or AR to provide immersive learning experiences. These technologies can be used for virtual field trips, science simulations, and more.
- Coding Games: Introduce them to basic programming concepts and simple computational thinking.
- Online Educational Videos, Digital Art, and Creativity Apps: Educational video platforms like YouTube Kids offer a wealth of age-appropriate videos on various subjects, including science experiments, storytelling, and math lessons. Explore their artistic talents through drawing, painting, and animation. It's a lot less messy when it's all online! *Please use parental controls on any device, including gaming systems, that your child may have access

to in your home. However, that alone is not failproof. It's been shown that even baby monitors can get hacked. Also, outside your home, don't assume that parental controls are used. It's essential to educate your child about the importance of not sharing personal information with strangers online.

Time Management:

Benefits: Helps develop a sense of routine and responsibility.

Activities:

- Visual Schedule: Create a visual daily schedule with pictures to help them understand and follow routines.
- Timed Activities: Use a timer or songs during activities like playtime, reading, and chores to teach time management.

Remember that kids learn best through play and hands-on experiences. Keep activities age and skill level appropriate. Provide plenty of positive reinforcement and encouragement as they develop these vital life skills.

Chapter 6

First Grade

First graders are at an age where they are eager to learn, and it's a great time to develop more foundational life skills. Teaching these skills early on can have a lasting positive impact on their personal growth and future success. Many life skills, such as organization, time management, and problem-solving, are transferable to the academic setting. Developing these skills early on can contribute to better school performance and a positive attitude towards learning.

Kids at this age are aware of how others perceive them. They may become more self-conscious. Build on the foundation of healthy life skills, eating habits, and being physically active rather than looking a certain way. Help your child navigate social situations and form meaningful connections with others.

Reinforce skills and add to them. Here are some appropriate life skills for first graders, along with the benefits of each skill and activities to implement them:

Communication Skills:

Benefits: Improved social interactions, better relationships, character development, and enhanced self-expression.

Activities:

- Reading: Set 20 minutes or more daily to read with your child. Read to them to strengthen their listening skills and patience. Have them practice their reading skills. Reading enhances vocabulary, expands access to knowledge, and is a fun bonding activity. It fosters curiosity and connection about the world around us. Let it be the gateway for further discussions. Build engagement by pausing and asking questions, have them predict what will happen next, and summarize the story. They will build critical thinking and comprehension skills.
- Storytelling: Tell a story emphasizing core values such as respect, honesty, patience, good manners, positive attitude, courage, and gratitude. Emphasize moments where characters exhibit these attributes. Have your child point out specific actions, words, or behaviors demonstrating these traits. Highlight consequences of poor behavior, such as missing out on an opportunity or getting in trouble to reinforce a lesson.
- Puppet Shows: Use puppets to act out scenarios that require communication and problem-solving. Talk about peer pressure and how they can always come to a parent for help. Describe attributes of a good friend and demonstrate ways to reciprocate friendship.

Cooking Skills:

Benefits: Promotes independence, healthy eating habits, and safety in the kitchen.

Activities:

- Garden Exploration: If you have a garden or access to one, involve your child in planting, caring for, and harvesting fruits or vegetables. The connection to their food source can make them more interested in trying fresh produce.

- Make Simple Appetizers: Have children help assemble fruit kabobs. They can choose the fruits. You can help them cut the fruits and choose fun-shaped cookie cutters to use. They can carefully thread the fruit onto skewers.
- Smoothies: Allow them to imagine and compile ingredients for a fruit smoothie. Help them use the blender with supervision. Taste test a variety and keep the good recipes. Obviously, be prepared to toss the gross samples!
- Yogurt Parfaits, Trail Mix, or Sundaes: Provide a variety of healthy ingredients like yogurt, granola, fruits, and nuts, and let your child create their own snack.
- Taste Test Game: Use a blindfold and have them guess what they are eating. Try to incorporate foods they like and some foods they've never tried. They can describe the smell, texture, and flavors. Have them sort what they like most to least.
- Science Project: Purposefully allow your food to change over time. Let your child to observe how a potato sprouts or a cut apple oxidizes. Discuss food safety.

Creativity and Artistic Expression:

Benefits: Uses imagination, self-expression, and fine motor skills. Able to explore interests and talents.

Activities:

- Drawing and Coloring: Search online for drawing tutorials or use books to expand their drawing and coloring skills. Artforkidshub.com is a favorite for many kids, and the library may have step-by-step drawing books to test out.
- Craft Projects: Engage in simple craft projects using everyday materials. Keep a supply handy after a dollar store outing, or squirrel away leftover paper towel rolls and other things you come across in your house. Tutorials online can help guide your child. You can purchase kits like Klutz, which offers a plethora of arts and crafts kits to choose from.

Oftentimes, your local craft stores will offer classes to help teach your kiddos; some even offer birthday party options!

Empathy and Kindness:

Benefits: Enhances social skills, emotional intelligence, and positive relationships. Teaching these values from a young age contributes to character development and ethical decision-making.

Activities:

- Story Reading: Read books that emphasize empathy and kindness. Find books online from your local library and schools offering online reading platforms like Epic and Sora. Storyline Online is another excellent resource where famous actors read engaging books.
- Acts of Kindness: Encourage them to perform small acts of kindness for others, such as opening the door, paying a compliment, or offering to help. Teach your child the importance of kindness, even when no one is watching.

Hygiene:

Benefits: Fosters healthy self-care habits and personal responsibility.

Activities:

- Bathtime routine: By now, your child may know how to take a bath or shower independently. Make sure they know which handles are used for hot and cold water, how to set the temperature, how much water to fill the bathtub, and how to open/close the drain. When showering, it's helpful to have a handheld showerhead with a water shut-off valve, but make sure they also know how to turn the water off completely. Emphasize the importance of cleaning all body parts. Gently remind your child to wash behind the ears, their belly buttons, and in between their toes. Especially if they do not use a 3-in-1 bottle or bar soap, it helps to keep containers consistent so that they know which is the body soap, shampoo, conditioner, and face soap. They should be able to dry themselves and put their wet towel back on the rack to dry, not on the floor! Lastly, starting with their underwear, they need to put all their clothes on independently.

- Hair Care: Besides using the right products, ensure they know how often they should wash their hair. Bonus if they can use a hair dryer. Dryer wands are easy to use and act as a brush. Remind them that they will need assistance plugging it in, never to use it around water, to maintain an arm's length distance when using a regular hair dryer to prevent hair from getting pulled into the dryer, and to keep moving to avoid heat damage. Encourage them to brush their hair regularly to prevent tangles, and consider braiding longer hair at bedtime. They can use a comb to part their hair. Have them practice gathering their hair, brushing it, and tying it all up in a ponytail without your supervision.
- Lotion: Depending on where you live, your child may need to use a moisturizing lotion. And no matter where you live, they should be accustomed to using sunscreen. The Australians use the saying, "Slip, slop, slap," which refers to slipping on a shirt, slopping on sunscreen, and slapping on a hat. It's a good motto for your kids to memorize when preparing for a day out. I prefer the coverage of a lathering lotion, but my husband likes the convenience of a spray. Either way, using sunscreen is essential. The more routine it is for them, the more willing they will be to try applying it themselves. Have them use a full-length mirror when applying themselves and supervise for ample coverage.
- Nail Care: Teach your child how to use a nail brush. Perfect for after they dig in the dirt during a gardening session! Don't forget the toes. Afterwards, trim and help them paint their nails.

Money Awareness:

Benefits: By gradually introducing money concepts, you are laying the groundwork for financial literacy and responsible money management.

Activities:

- Play Bank: Create a pretend bank where they can use play money. Practice being the teller and customer. Ask to change a $50 bill into smaller bills that equal the same amount. Deposit paper money and have them count it out. Perhaps go to your bank with your child to open an account for them, if they don't have one. Teach the importance of saving for a larger goal.
- Board Games: If they show interest in board games, play games that require the use of fake money. Help them be the banker.
- Cashier: Basic math concepts are still being learned at this age. Have them recognize if change is due when making a purchase. Start simple and mix it up as they show progress.
- Sorting: Sort coins by type. Learn the different names and values of the coins. Have them count pennies by 1s, nickels by 5s, dimes by 10s, and quarters by 25s. If you have access to other coins or find them online, you can show that we have half dollars and dollar coins, as well. You could show them how to roll change and exchange the coins for paper bills at a bank. If you're short on time, show them how a coin-counting machine works. Keep a few quarters out to try out the small toy or candy machines. They will not forget the value of quarters and will think they are rich!

Organizational Skills:

Benefits: Reduces clutter, improves efficiency, and reduces stress.

Activities:

- Toy Roundup: Encourage your child to consider donating or selling unused items. They can go with you to a donation center and perhaps thrift a reward. You can also teach them how to take pictures of their goods for you to post online. Have them decide how much to price an item. This can be a reasonable amount. Teach them how to research similarly priced used items or sell their item at a discount that is ½ the price of a similar, new product.

- Backpack Organization: Help them keep their school backpacks tidy and organized. Teach them that everything has a home so that they can find things when they need them. Finished homework should promptly be put back in their backpack. It really sucks to put forth the effort in doing homework only to find it's not in their bag when it comes time to turn it in. They should also be responsible for keeping their backpack clean, both inside and out. That applies to their lunch bag, too!

Problem Solving:

Benefits: Enhances critical thinking and decision-making skills. Begin to understand that their actions have consequences and that they are accountable for their choices and behavior. Learn how to approach challenges, find solutions, and adapt to different situations.

Activities:

- Puzzles and Games: Offer age-appropriate puzzles and games that require problem-solving. Introduce your child to simple Lego kits where they have to follow instructions. Tangrams are great for pattern recognition. You can use physical puzzle pieces, play online or through an app like Osmo.
- Brain Teasers: Present riddles or brain teasers for them to solve. Have them memorize some for their classmates and friends. Can they think of one to stump you?
- "What If" Scenarios: Discuss hypothetical scenarios and encourage them to come up with solutions. Follow up with "What else?" to get them to diversify their answers.
- Emotions: Talk about different emotions we have. Have your child think of what causes certain emotions. Empower

your child with self-regulation techniques. Practice ways to help regulate emotions like anger and nervousness by counting, deep breathing, taking a break, or slowly counting up to a certain number. Help your child find ways to manage their emotions, especially when you are not around to help them.

- Flying a Kite: Help your child pick out and buy a kite. Plan a windy day outing in an open field, away from power lines. Show them how to fly it, switching directions and running if need be while paying attention to their surroundings and reeling the kite out and in. Try to avoid hard crashes, people, and other pitfalls.

Physical Fitness:

Benefits: Promotes a healthy lifestyle and physical development. Establish goals and work towards accomplishing them. Have them practice for improvements. Teach them to be resilient when facing challenges.

Activities:

- Outdoor Play: Encourage active outdoor play like biking, running, or playing ball. You could set up relay races or obstacle courses. Use a timer and have them try to beat their own time or race another person. Don't give up; lose with grace, and keep practicing.
- Yoga for Kids: Introduce basic yoga poses and stretches suitable for their age. There are online tutorials specific for kids that have story themes, or you may be able to find family yoga classes in your community.

Responsibility:

Benefit: Instills moral and ethical principles. It lays a foundation for raising capable individuals, reducing their reliance on adults for basic tasks. Responsible individuals are generally more reliable and trust-worthy, making them better friends, family members, and team players in school and extracurricular activities.

Activities:

- Cleaning: Teach your child about the differences in cleaners and how to store them properly. Give them simple chores that they'll still find fun. As children successfully complete tasks and responsibilities, they gain a sense of accomplishment and self-worth. This boosts their self-esteem and confidence.
- Mail: Supervise your child checking the mail or putting mail in the mailbox. Teach your child the basics of how to address an envelope or box. Send artwork to the grandparents. Have them put the stamp on. You could have your child help with an Amazon return. Watch videos online to see how mail is processed and take them with you to the post office to see how the mail person weighs mail and receives payment.

Safety Awareness:

Benefits: Ensures their safety in various situations. Learn how to assess situations, weigh options, and make informed choices. Better recognize and respond to potential risks.

Activities:

- Safety Drills, Stranger Danger, and Setting Boundaries: Act out your family safety escape plans, refresh your kids to be aware of stranger danger, and remind your child about inappropriate touches. Keep your kids alert and informed. Let them know you are always available to listen and help.
- Open Communication: Maintain open and honest communication with your child. As they get older, it only gets more important. Practice your listening skills here, and don't be overly critical. Encourage them to ask questions and express any concerns.
- True/False Safety Rules: Establish clear safety rules at home, such as always wearing a helmet when riding a bike or not opening the door to strangers. Make sure your child

knows the importance of not playing with matches or lighters. The use of any power outlets should be off-limits. Be consistent with your rules, or they will not be taken seriously. There should be consequences for not obeying the rules you set for their safety.

- Visit Safety Resources: Call your local fire stations or police departments to see if you can arrange a visit to learn about safety equipment and meet safety professionals. Your school may even set up a field trip. Homeschoolers have extra time to incorporate local resources. In advance, let your child know you'll want to hear about what they learned so that they'll be paying attention during the visit. Make sure you ask questions and have an open discussion as a follow-up.

Technology:

Benefits: Enhance cognitive learning and development.

Activities:

- Music: Learn to play an instrument without the stress of learning how to read sheet music. You can use apps or buy a keyboard that lights up to learn how to play. Your child will work to memorize an entire song and work towards developing more creative skills.
- Typing: Find free typing games online to learn the keys and improve typing accuracy on sites like Typing.com
- Language: The younger brains have an easier time learning languages. Apps like Duolingo use audio prompts and pictures with cartoon characters to make learning a language fun. You can also find native language speakers offering online classes. It's a small world, after all.

Telling time:

Benefits: Encourages responsibility and punctuality.

Activities:

- Flash Cards: Make flashcards that will show the passage of time. Have your child put them in order, showing what happens first and next. Then move on to yesterday, today, tonight, tomorrow, the past, present, and future.
- Timed Tasks: Set a timer for activities like brushing their teeth, cleaning their room, completing an obstacle course, showering, or completing homework.
- Daily Schedule: Create a visual daily schedule to help them manage their time. A chart can include their entire day or be more specific to getting ready for school, getting ready for bedtime, or scheduling activities to complete.
- Calendar: Print out a monthly calendar to give to them each month. Help them mark important birthdays and events with stickers or drawings. Discuss holidays and upcoming events. They can also work on time in relation to a full calendar, such as days of the week, weekdays, weekends, months, and seasons. Talk about how they dress for different times of the year.
- Digital Clock: Teach your child how to read and use a digital clock. Play around with the hours and minutes. Have them set a specific time or read the time to you. Set the alarm.
- Analog clock: Make a paper plate clock with moveable hands. Start by teaching the hours with the short hand. Then, add the long hand to show the minutes. Practice first for hours and 30 minutes. Show how the short-hour hand moves towards the following number. Once they are comfortable, you can practice 5-minute increments and to the minute. Write digital times on a flashcard and help your child show the correct time on the plate. Discuss vocabulary such as am, pm, and o'clock. Consider more advanced words like half-past, quarter past, and quarter to as they develop. Buy them a watch to practice telling time. You'll want to remind them to be extra careful with it when it comes time to wash their hands.

- Counting: Point to the notches on an analog clock and count to 60. Practice skip counting by 5's. Show the difference between hours, minutes, and seconds.
- Q&A: Use everyday scenarios to practice telling time, such as meal times, bedtime, and school start times. Ask your child questions like, "When do you eat breakfast?" or "What happens at noon?" Ask them to report the time to you throughout the day to reinforce learning. They'll love being helpful!

It's important to remember that kids learn best through hands-on experiences and play. These activities should be age-appropriate, enjoyable, and designed to encourage active participation. As they develop these life skills, children become more motivated to explore and adapt to new experiences. Empower your child to become capable, responsible, and well-rounded individuals who can navigate the challenges and opportunities they encounter. They'll gain confidence and a greater sense of independence to better interact with the world around them.

Chapter 7

Second Grade

Second graders are becoming more independent, able to take on more chores, and are still eager to be helpful. They enjoy trying new things and are more involved with their family and friends. They may get bored by not knowing how to use their energy and may still need a lot of guidance. Help them work their way to more independence.

Here are some appropriate life skills for second graders, along with their benefits and activities to teach and reinforce these skills:

Cleaning and Organization:

Benefits: Encourages responsibility in contributing to the household and pride in living in a clean environment. Promotes respect for property and organization.

Activities:

- Chores: Expand their chores to include wiping down countertops/tables, straightening up the bathroom after use, especially changing the toilet paper roll, and making their bed. They can learn to pull up their sheets, blankets and arrange their pillows. Beddy's Bedding and similar brands make it super easy to make a bed, especially for bunk beds and RVs, with their easy-to-make zippered beddings. Dirty dishes can be rinsed and put in the dishwasher. Have them add detergent and start the wash when it's full. You'll need to wait until they are a bit taller to put away the clean dishes, but they might be able to manage the utensils. While the jobs may not be perfectly done, it teaches them basic tidiness. As the world implies, they may start to not enjoy chores, but they'll appreciate rewards!

- Feeding Pets: If you have pets, second graders can take on the responsibility of feeding them. Teach them the proper portion sizes and schedules.
- Laundry: Check clothes for stains, rips, and missing buttons with assistance. Discuss common laundry cleaning supplies such as detergent, stain removers, and drying sheets. Have them measure the appropriate amount of laundry detergent to add to the washer. Discuss the various laundry detergent types and the amount needed to be used based on machines and the amount of clothes being washed. Have them gather the clothes from the dryer and clean the lint tray. You could read or watch a video on the evolution of washing clothes through to dry cleaning. Next time you are in a museum or antique show, point out the washboard. Practice gratitude for modern washers and dryers; some people in other parts of the world are not so lucky! Talk about the difference between using a dryer or hanging delicates to dry. Expand on their basic sorting and matching. While they may not fold perfectly, kids can fold small items like washcloths, hand towels, and socks.
- Labeling: Teach your child to label and organize their school supplies, clothing, and toys. Discuss the consequences of misplacing or mistreating belongings.

Cooking Skills:

Benefits: Teaches independence, nutrition, and following instructions.

Activities:

- Pouring: This can be a nerve-racking process, but your child should be able to pour a drink independently. Have them practice with cereal and milk into a bowl and work up to pouring drinks into cups. When they spill, have them clean it up. They will learn to be more careful and less reluctant to spill in the future.
- Kitchen Tools: Use kitchen tools with assistance, such as a peeler, apple slicer, or can opener. Supervise them cutting their own food and grating cheese for taco night or a homemade pizza. Use a toaster with tongs, microwave with mitts to make simple snacks, and make drinks in a blender with minimal assistance. Supervise them making avocado toast and hot chocolate in the microwave or using a mixer to help bake a cake.
- Practice Safety: Find safety issues in the kitchen, such as the electrical cord being too close to water.
- Simple Meals: Use the stove and oven with adult supervision. Warm up soup on the stove. Practice making scrambled eggs. Have them crack the egg, whip it, and cook in a heated pan. Make sure they understand the importance of safety while cooking and that it should only be done while supervised. Eat it on its own or in a sandwich. They can make a healthy side salad to go with it.
- Store food: Have them put leftovers in appropriate containers and store them in the pantry or refrigerator. Discuss how to identify spoiled food and find the best use date.
- Easy Bake Oven: Gift them their very own oven, a true classic, the Easy-Bake! The company recommends the product for ages 8+. My kids loved following the directions, measuring ingredients, making miniature baked goods, and putting the finishing touches on their treats. You may not be overly impressed by the process, but they'll have fun!

Money Skills:

Benefits: Promotes money management skills.

Activities:

- Where to shop: Take your child shopping at various stores. Identify the kinds of stores that sell certain items. Pretend you need something. Have your child choose a store that sells what you need.
- Shopping at Markets: Teach your child how to support local and buy fresh food from farmers and homemade crafts from vendors. Some may only take cash purchases. Take your child to your bank or ATM and have them help withdraw cash.
- Entrepreneurship: Follow up on the shopping trip by teaching a bit about entrepreneurship. Have your child brainstorm ideas for their own business. Help them set up an online shop or have them sell at a local craft market. They could even start with a neighborhood lemon stand or sell cookies as a Girl Scout.

Problem-Solving:

Benefits: Develops critical thinking and decision-making skills.

Activities:

- Brainstorming: Encourage communication and listen to their issues without interjecting your solutions. Help them brainstorm solutions to everyday problems or peaceful resolutions to minor disagreements with siblings and friends.
- Battery Identification: Learn the common types of batteries, know how to find the correct size to replace in toys, and know when to replace/recharge. Discuss how to conserve energy by turning off items not in use and the consequences of not doing so. Ask for assistance changing batteries or plugging into a charger for electronic devices.
- Mapping and Pokemon GO: Learn how to use a physical map and GPS. Where are they on the map, and where do

they want to go? Look for landmarks to help with orientation and identify them, as well as street names, along commonly traveled routes. Know the difference between right and left. Understand cardinal directions such as north, south, east, and west. Have your child practice asking for directions. Have them guide you home on a walk or in the car. Consider a fun way to bridge technology with their basic mapping skills by playing an augmented reality game, like Pokemon Go, with your child. There are tutorials available online to get your family started.

Safety Skills:

Benefits: Prepared in an emergency situation. Plan in advance.

Activities:

- Safety Drill: Along with knowing how to exit a building, they should know how to put out a small fire, especially when learning to cook. Show them where the fire extinguisher is stored and how to use it.
- Heimlich Maneuver: Teach your child to recognize when someone is choking. It is recommended that kids as young as seven learn how to use the life-saving technique. Although in most emergencies, an adult is preferred, children can take a virtual class at heimlichheroes.com/virtual-learning-lessons and use their knowledge in life-or-death situations. Alternatively, you could search for hands-on training programs that cater to children in your local area.

Setting and Achieving Goals:

Benefits: Develops motivation, perseverance, and a sense of accomplishment.

Activities:

- Short-term goals: Help them set achievable goals, such as finishing a book or stopping a bad habit, like biting nails.

Celebrate their successes and encourage them to set new goals.

- Lessons: Learn to play a new instrument or the fundamentals of a sport.

Sewing Skills:

Benefits: Fosters creativity, problem-solving, and fine motor skills:

Activities:

- Fix a shirt: Teach them how to thread a needle and sew on buttons.
- Arts & Crafts: Create simple sewing projects like making a felt bookmark or decorating a cloth bag.

Social Skills:

Benefits: It allows kids to interact positively with others and communicate their needs, wants, and feelings effectively.

Activities:

- Writing: Find a pen pal, learn the structure of a formal letter, write a short letter or e-mail, send a thank you note, address an envelope
- Birthdays: Have them make or buy a card and gifts. They can learn how to wrap a present, use ribbons, and make their own bows. Look for online tutorials for a wealth of gift-wrapping videos.
- Phone Etiquette: Although you may no longer have a house phone and your child doesn't own a cell phone, it's beneficial to learn how to answer the phone and leave a thorough message. You can role-play with walkie-talkies! Have them listen, take notes on important information, repeat information back to the caller, speak slowly, and leave a detailed message stating their name, reason for calling, and their callback number. Also, speak with a smile. It really does change the tone of the conversation.

You can almost hear the smile come through on the other end.

- Ordering Food: Next time your family wants takeout, have your child compile an order and have them use the speaker phone to call in an order.
- Compliments: Practice giving and receiving compliments. This can be awkward for some, so practice making it normal behavior.
- Brainstorming Manners: Ask them, " What should you do if a door is closed? How do you get an adult's attention? Why is it rude to speak while others are speaking? How should we chew food when we eat? What should you do if you want a toy that another kid is playing with?" Kids need reminders and practice.
- Peer Pressure Role Play: Set up different scenarios to see how your child reacts. Keep open communication with your child. You can always be their reason for not doing something, "My parents won't let me." Tell your child that it is okay to walk away if they feel uncomfortable or unsafe. Be their excuse for removing themselves from a bad situation, "My parents are on their way to pick me up. Gotta go!" Teach them to be assertive in peer-pressure situations. Building self-confidence and self-esteem can help children feel better about themselves and their decisions.
- Discuss ways to detect and avoid being bullied. Bullies often seek a reaction and call out a kid who is alone. Your child can try to ignore the situation and remain calm. Do not show fear or anger in front of a bully. They can try to diffuse a situation by using humor. Enrolling in self-defense classes can help kids build physical and mental confidence, although this should not be a primary strategy for dealing with bullying. Ensure your child knows when assistance is needed and how to find it. If there is an unmanageable bully, have them report incidents to teachers, principals, or school counselors. Watch for changes in your child. Severe emotional distress, anxiety, or depression may need professional help from a therapist or counselor. Extreme

cases of physical bullying or threats may necessitate involvement from law enforcement. Bullying should be taken seriously.

Time Management:

Benefits: Helps with prioritizing tasks, punctuality, and a sense of responsibilities when completing tasks.

Activities:

- Homework Schedule: Create a homework schedule that includes designated time for completing homework assignments. Avoid procrastinating and discuss the consequences. Time shouldn't be left open-ended as it's not only essential to finish their homework but to be efficient in getting it done. Remind them that as they get older, completing their work during a test is just as crucial as getting the correct answers. If they don't finish on time, the answers they may have known will simply be marked wrong because they didn't manage their time. This may apply in elementary school, where they may not get to go to recess or have extra homework if they don't finish on time. Make it a consistent part of their daily routine.
- Task Prioritization Game: Play a game where they rank tasks in order of importance or urgency. For example, they can decide whether finishing homework or cleaning their room should come first.
- Cooking: Have them manage their time to follow a recipe. Explain the importance of timing in cooking.
- Clock Reading Practice: Practice reading analog clocks and telling time. Use fun activities like "What time will it be in 30 minutes?" to reinforce time concepts.
- Escape Rooms: You'll need to check with age requirements, but time management is exciting when playing in a group escape room. Check Groupon for group discounts with family or friends.

These life skills and activities are both educational and mostly enjoyable for second graders. It's essential to provide clear instructions and supervise them until they become familiar with the tasks. Make chores a part of their routine and avoid overwhelming them with too many responsibilities at once. Praise and acknowledge their efforts to reinforce their sense of accomplishment and responsibility.

Chapter 8

Third Grade

Third grade can be a challenging time for kids and their families. Your child has moved into a new tier at elementary school. Third through fifth graders are now upper elementary students. They will be expected to do their work more independently, requiring more focus for extended periods of time. State and national standardized testing starts in third grade. Your child must be more responsible, efficient with time management skills, and focused. Depending on your school, they may have subtle changes like a different play area from the younger kids for recess, use of separate bathrooms, or transition to A-F letter grades on tests and report cards. This may also be a benchmark year where their school performance leads to a fourth-grade promotion or retention in third.

Third graders are better at analyzing situations, making informed decisions, and finding creative solutions to challenges they encounter. They are learning to take ownership of their actions by understanding the consequences of their choices and the impacts of their decisions. This is a good age to start working on more long-term goals for the future and developing crucial decision-making skills. These skills are an investment in their well-rounded development, their ability to pursue higher-level education, and community involvement.

Here are some appropriate life skills for third graders, along with their benefits and activities to practice skills:

Communication:

Benefits: Enhances interpersonal relationships and conflict resolution.

Activities:

- Listening: Encourage active listening by having meaningful conversations with your child. Relate the importance of eye contact, not interrupting, and non-verbal cues like nodding their head for comprehension.
- Presentations: Have them rehearse any presentations with you. Give positive feedback and discuss areas for improvement. They can practice in front of a mirror, as well. Teach them to memorize the content and only use their notes for reference. Have them use hand gestures and facial expressions to help convey their message.
- Friends: Teach them to express their thoughts and feelings respectfully. Have them practice using "I" statements to express their feelings. For example, instead of saying, "You make me mad," they can say, "I feel upset when..." "I" statements help put the focus on their own feelings and experiences rather than on what the other person has done or failed to do. Explain that body language, facial expressions, and tone of voice all convey emotions. Encourage them to be aware of these cues in themselves and others. Encourage patience when waiting for their turn to speak. Teach them that it's okay to express their thoughts and feelings but that they should also listen to others.
- Journaling: Provide a journal or notebook where children can write or draw their thoughts and feelings. This can be a private outlet for self-expression.
- Signature: Most kids learn cursive in the third grade. Teach them how to sign their name. Have them practice at the end of a written letter. Tell them it'll come in handy if they need to write a check, sign for a package, or sign legal documents.

Cooking:

Benefits: Promotes independence, nutrition awareness, healthy eating, and following instructions.

Activities:

- Themed meal: Have them think of a meal they'd like to prepare from a particular country or for a holiday. Help them prepare dishes, conveying kitchen safety and the importance of following recipes. Have them read the entire directions prior to starting. Make up a grocery list and take them shopping if needed. Teach them how to substitute or when it's acceptable to omit ingredients.
- Nutrition: Teach them to read food labels and make informed decisions about what they eat. What should they avoid? What is good for them? Have them plan a balanced, nutritious meal. In advance, prepare healthier snacks like pre-washed and cut-up fruits and vegetables for when hunger strikes.
- Shopping Scavenger Hunt: Always start with a grocery list so they don't forget what they need to buy. We've all been there. Consider setting a budget. Teach them the general grocery store layout. Inform them to focus on shopping in healthier areas, generally towards the outer walls and not the aisles. Show them the cold section, canned areas, and drink aisles. Have them ask a store clerk if they can't find something. Your child can practice reading the aisle descriptions to quickly access ingredients vs. perusing down all the aisles to avoid unnecessary purchases.

Environmental Awareness:

Benefits: Instills the importance of sustainable practices and encourages them to be stewards of the environment.

Activities:

- Community Service: Participate in community clean-ups. This could be at a park, beach, on a trail, at school, or around the neighborhood.
- Outing: Explore local nature centers, botanical gardens, a zoo, or science museums with exhibits related to conservation. These provide opportunities for hands-on learning. Consider volunteering.
- Scavenger Hunt: Create a list of items commonly found in nature, like leaves, rocks, or animal tracks. Go to a park or on a hike to find and identify these items.
- Eco-friendly Composting: Teach kids about composting and involve them in the process. Set up a compost bin for food scraps and yard waste, and explain how composting reduces waste and enriches soil.
- Plant a Garden: Involve kids in planting and caring for a garden, whether it's a small vegetable plot, flower garden, or container garden. Collect rainwater for watering plants. Share the harvest with neighbors, family, and friends. Teach them about the importance of nurturing plants and their environmental role.
- Energy Conservation: Conduct an energy audit of your home with kids. Identify areas where energy can be saved, such as turning off lights and appliances when not in use and sealing drafts. Teach them to conserve resources and save money.
- Movies: Watch age-appropriate documentaries or movies focusing on conservation and environmental issues. Discuss the content and its implications. Subscription packages on Disney+ include National Geographic.

Self-care and Hygiene:

Benefits: Instills responsibility and pride in oneself.

- Eyewear: Have your child correctly store and clean their glasses. If they require glasses for school, remind them to wear them when needed. Sunglasses are just as crucial for protecting their eyes.

- Clean ears: Supervise them using a cotton swab to clean the outside and gently around the inner canal.
- Self-confidence and self-esteem:
- Posture: Encourage good posture when standing and sitting.
- Scale: Show them how to use a scale. Although not always consistently accurate, some scales can estimate more than weight. It is helpful to discuss body fat, body mass index (BMI), muscle mass, water retention, heart rate, and other factors that pop up on the reading.

Money Management:

Benefits: Builds financial literacy and responsible money handling.

Activities:

- Goal: Help them create saving,s short and long-term goals, and encourage them to save part of their allowance or gifts.
- Garage Sale: Clear out the house and help your child sell unused and unwanted items.

Problem-Solving:

Benefits: Develops critical thinking and decision-making skills.

Activities:

- Games: Present them with a Rubix cube or chess board. Teach them how to play, have them learn various strategies with you or online, and encourage them to practice.
- Multiplication Bingo: Create Bingo cards with multiplication problems instead of numbers. Call out multiplication equations (e.g., 3 x 4) and have the kids mark the answers on their Bingo cards.
- Math Fact Flashcards: Create flashcards with multiplication and division facts. You can make these yourself or find printable ones online. To keep the stack organized, punch a hole in each card, attach them to a ring like a keychain, and have them flip through for

memorization. Have your child practice with the flashcards daily for a few minutes.

- Math Story Problems: Create story problems that involve multiplication and division. For example, "Sally has 24 candies and wants to share them equally with four friends. How many candies does each friend get?" This helps kids understand real-life applications of these math operations. You can use manipulatives such as coins, beans, or other items found around the house.
- Math Riddles: Present your child with math riddles or brain teasers that involve multiplication and division. For instance, "I am thinking of a number. When I multiply it by 5 and then subtract 10, I get 30. What is my number?" Teach them how to work backward from the answer to find the solution. Keep scrap paper and a pencil handy, as numbers can get confusing!
- Brainstorming: Use everyday situations to encourage solutions to problems. They tend to use the word bored more and more. Help them think of ways to spend their time. Before the long summer holiday, work with them to write out a list of all that they would like to do and have a checklist for them to cross off. This can also be a motivator to work towards some goals.
- Food and drinks: Have your child decide what they would like to eat and have them order their food. Show them how to use a vending machine.
- Mapping Skills for Hunts: Work with your child to look for local caches on the internet, such as geocaching.com. Choose an easy cache for your first hunt. Caches have ratings on difficulty, size, and terrain. Have your child practice using a GPS to find coordinates. Once found, consider setting one up for other players. Or consider taking turns doing a mapped-out scavenger hunt. Leave clues from one location to the next.

Reading:

Benefits: Enhances communication, vocabulary, and critical thinking.

Activities:

- Critical-thinking Comprehension: Encourage regular reading of age-appropriate books across different genres. Have them distinguish beyond fiction and non-fiction, such as a legend, fairytale, biography, autobiography, etc. Discuss the stories with your child. In previous years, your child was learning to read. You'll find the focus now to be reading to learn. Use comprehension exercises like asking them to summarize a story, determine the main idea (oftentimes, it relates to a lesson learned), and supporting details. They will need to learn how to read between the lines. Discuss any figurative language that implies something. Compare and contrast two short stories. How are they similar and different? When discussing cause and effect, remind them that they do not always come in order. Ask both specific and open-ended questions. Have your child draw their own conclusions by making inferences beyond the end of a story.
- Testing: Practice reading or discussing questions prior to reading. This is an important test-taking skill that will have them actively reading and listening. While not always an option, if they know the questions in advance, they can find answers as they read or listen. This can help with their time management during tests to avoid re-reading a passage to find answers at the end.

Responsibility:

Benefits: Helps become more independent and take care of things and tasks on their own.

Activities:

- Homework: This is a vital time to transition from doing homework together to checking homework that is done independently. You will not be there for your child during tests at school. Your child needs to understand the directions and complete an assignment independently.

They will need to learn how to manage their time while completing their homework and lessons in school. Remind them that during a test, time is important. Even if they may have known the answers, if they don't complete their work on time, the questions will be marked wrong. Try to remove distractions but also let them know that their work needs to be completed regardless of distractions. They will need to learn how to focus. Review their assignment and discuss improvements. Relate the importance of checking their work when they have time, as they should during a test. They may have the correct answers but have careless mistakes. Most unfamiliar words they need to spell will be referenced in the text. Have them check for correct spelling, capitalization, and punctuation. By not holding your child's hand during assignments, you will learn areas where your child may need more help and guide them in those areas.

- Outdoor Toys: Teach your child how to maintain their bike. Show them how to change a tire and how to use a pump. Have them practice inflating balls. Remind them to keep their outdoor toys clean and organized. Discuss what happens if toys are left unintended or how they can rust if left outside in the rain or snow.
- Chores: Have them gather the trash and place it in the bin before trash day. Make it their responsibility. Help them put the trash bin out for pick up. Help clean up outside the home by raking up leaves or shoveling snow.
- Pet and plant care: Start with role-modeling care with a stuffed animal or other toys. Practice feeding, bathing, and cleaning up after a pet. Consider fostering an animal, pet sitting for a neighbor, or getting a pet. If a pet seems like too much, start with a plant. Be sure to remind your child of the importance of fulfilling commitments. Caring for others and fulfilling an obligation fosters empathy and consideration for the needs and feelings of all living things.

Time Management:

Benefits: Enhances organization, punctuality, and task completion.

Activities:

- Calendar Planner: Introduce a weekly planner or calendar for them to schedule homework, extracurricular activities, and playtime. Have them choose a planner book, some planning stickers, and colorful pens. Let them organize their schedules and keep track of important assignments. They can color code homework, activities, holidays, and birthdays.
- Alarms: Have them set their own alarms for school or reading time. Discuss the importance of managing time efficiently.
- Homework: If you haven't already, establish a designated homework space and time. Have your child keep the area clean and organized after each use. Teach them effective study strategies like note-taking and, if possible, reading the questions prior to a passage. Have them pinpoint what information they are searching for and manage their time more efficiently. Also, reiterate the importance of not procrastinating, especially on projects that are not due immediately. That will help them manage any unnecessary stress.

Remember to adapt these activities to your child's skill level and provide guidance and encouragement as they practice. Regular practice and a variety of engaging activities help reinforce these essential skills. Be supportive, but don't be a helicopter parent!

Chapter 9

Fourth Grade

Help fourth graders establish a strong sense of themselves. Promote self-awareness, self-esteem, and a sense of identity. Practice critical thinking and problem-solving, which are essential for handling challenges and making informed decisions. Encourage responsible behavior, decision-making, and taking ownership of one's actions. Empower fourth graders to become more accountable and self-reliant.

Set clear expectations for behavior and responsibility. They learn through example, so practice what you preach. Involve the whole family in learning and practicing life skills. Create a supportive environment where everyone participates. Be consistent in teaching and reinforcing life skills. Consistency helps children establish routines and habits. Show the relevance of life skills in their daily lives. Emphasize that life skills are not just for now but how they will benefit them as they grow and face new challenges in the future.

Give them opportunities to practice regularly. Encourage children to learn from their mistakes. Mistakes are part of the learning process, and they should understand that it's okay to not be perfect. Gradually allow them more independence and responsibility as they demonstrate their ability to handle it. Teach them to reflect on their actions and decisions. Help them identify what went well and areas they can improve upon.

By taking these approaches into consideration, parents, caregivers, and educators can effectively teach fourth graders valuable life skills. Here are some essential life skills for fourth graders, along with their benefits and activities to reinforce learning:

Communication:

Benefits: Have your child practice asking relevant questions and have them seek clarification when needed. By becoming more proficient in communication, they gain confidence in expressing themselves, which can positively impact their self-esteem and self-confidence.

Activities:

- Health: Describe symptoms of injury or illness to a nurse or doctor. Teach them to know and share, with a medical professional, their own health information regarding allergies, medications, or past complications. Have them identify locations to receive medications, such as a school nurse or purchases at a pharmacy. Explain why adult supervision is required before taking medications. Ask your child if they want to swallow a pill vs drinking liquid medication. Teach them that some medications require a prescription from their doctor while others do not. You can discuss the different doctors they see, such as their primary pediatrician, optometrist, and dentist. Further discussions can lead to being familiar with the name of their insurance and their medical group.
- Board Games: Play Scrabble, Boggle, or Pictionary, which require effective communication, vocabulary, and strategic thinking.
- Listening to Podcasts: Listen to age-appropriate podcasts together and discuss the content. This promotes active listening and critical thinking.

Financial Literacy:

Benefits: Teaches money management, budgeting, and responsible spending.

Activities:

- Budget Game: Give your child a set amount of money for a gift-giving holiday for the family. Have them set a budget for each family member and come up with thoughtful gift ideas. Brainstorm each person's interests, needs, and wants. Order gifts online or take your child to a store to purchase gifts. Bonus: If they stay under the set amount given, they get to keep whatever is left over.
- Sell Online: Learn how to sell something online. Have your child factor in pricing to consider what the final product should cost. Would it be more cost-effective to resale something or start from scratch? Reselling their used clothes and shoes is an easy way to start, or they may have a good idea for making a new product.
- Shopping: Go to a dollar store and have them choose a few to purchase. Have them estimate the amount of the entire purchase and determine if they have enough money to buy everything. Put back what they can't afford. Pay the exact amount for purchases at a store. (Bring plenty of change.) Count change to make sure it is accurate, and have them practice checking the receipt as well.

Goal skills:

Benefits: Gives a sense of purpose and motivation. Clear objectives help kids focus on their tasks and work diligently to achieve them. Children learn to take ownership of their actions and work towards their objectives, promoting a sense of accountability. Pursuing goals often involves overcoming obstacles and setbacks. They understand the value of persistence and resilience.

Activities:

- Fun Run: Set up a goal for the end of the year to run a race. Break down the goal into four manageable quarterly goals, three months each of focused effort. Start by walking around the block once a week. Then, for the second and third quarters, you could have your child focus on increasing time or distance. For the last quarter, combine all the effort and sign up for a local 5K Fun Run. This can be a fun activity for the whole family, and you are not required to run the entire time. Volunteers and spectators cheer you on during the run. Usually, there are snacks and drinks, a finisher's shirt, and a medal for runners at the end of the race.

- Time Capsule: Have your child create a time capsule, including a letter to their future selves. Where are they in life now, and what do they want to accomplish when they retrieve the capsule? This activity teaches reflection and future goal-setting.
- Camping Trip: Help them plan a camping trip. Figure out where to go and what to bring. Perhaps access the supplies you have on hand vs. what they'll need to get. Ask the family who would like to join and figure out some dates that might work. Check the weather forecast and book the trip. Find campsite openings by calling or looking on reservation sites. Help them organize supplies, food, and entertainment. You could teach them how to fish if you are near water, practice survival skills like starting a fire, learn how to put up a tent, make s'mores without burning or losing the marshmallows, store food away from potential animals, cook a meal on a campfire and conserve resources while still practicing good hygiene.

Home skills:

Benefits: Gain confidence in their abilities to become more self-sufficient.

Activities:

- Sewing Kits: Fun doll and animal kits teach basic stitches. They can be purchased online and at craft stores. Upcycle clothes. If you have some old clothes, rather than tossing them, have your child practice designing and stitching with the material.

- Chores: Your child can be responsible for mopping the floors and helping you clean the cars, both inside and out. Have them check to see if the dishwasher is clean before putting the dishes away. They can set aside dishes for you on the counter for harder-to-reach places.
- Meal: Set nights where your child has more time to help you prepare meals. Your child will see firsthand how to cook and plan breakfasts, lunches, and dinners. Incorporate their help wherever you can. This helps them develop an appreciation for the effort that goes into meal preparation. They are more likely to value food and reduce food waste when they have firsthand experience in the kitchen.

Navigational skills:

Benefits: Improves a child's spatial awareness and understanding of their physical surroundings. They can better understand the world around them, including continents, countries, states, and landmarks. They will need to analyze information, make decisions about directions, and adapt to changing circumstances.

Activities:

- Bike Ride: Practice using a paper map and GPS. Have them search for and choose a local bike route or create one. Tell them there might not be cell service in the area and to mark the trail on a map and make sure they bring it with them. Go on a family bike ride with your child as the guide.
- Public Transportation: Have them plan a family activity only using public transportation. Use a bus or rail system. Show them how to use apps to estimate travel time and compare various transportation options. Teach them how to rent a scooter or driver through an app.

- Travel: Learn how to identify cities, states, and countries on a map in relation to their home. With your help, have them map out and plan a day for sightseeing. Plan the logistics.

Responsibilities:

Benefits: Learning to manage tasks and make decisions on their own contributes to their self-sufficiency and boosts self-confidence.

Activities:

- Sleepover: Invite a friend to sleepover. Brainstorm experiences that they both would enjoy. Have your child plan potential activities, where and how they will sleep, and any meals that might be involved. Teach them to be flexible and accountable.
- Hanging out: Know where your child is, how you can find them, and whether a responsible adult is present. Set a pick-up time or time you expect them to be home. Have your child call you for any reason and have a way to reach your child.
- Lunch: Keep a school lunch calendar on the fridge. Over the weekend, have your child decide the days they would like to eat at school or pack their own lunch. In advance, have them plan what they will make for home-brought lunch and add to the grocery list if needed. Show them how you keep track of their school account funds. When the meal account is low, have them deposit cash if that is an option.
- Library: Get your child a local library card, or let them borrow yours. Have them be more responsible for keeping track of the books and organizing them when they are due. Let them take the lead for returning books or paying the fine for being late.

Teamwork and Collaboration:

Benefits: Enhances social skills, cooperation, and the ability to work effectively with others while forming interests.

Activities:

- Group Work: Engage in group projects outside of school, such as joining a volunteer group, team sports, special interests club like robotics, or an organized troop that requires collaboration.
- Book Club: Start or join a book club where kids read the same book and discuss it together. This activity promotes critical thinking and discussion skills.

Technological skills

Benefits: Prepares your child for the modern world and enhances their educational experiences. It helps children locate, evaluate, and utilize information from various sources.

Activities:

- Photography and videography: Learn to edit images, save different file formats, and print.
- Coding and Programming: Learning the basics of coding and programming introduces your child to computational thinking and problem-solving, which are valuable skills for the future. Find interactive online platforms that use block-based coding, making it easy for beginners to create animations and games. Examples include Scratch, Code.org, and Tynker.
- Robotics Kits: Explore robotics kits like LEGO Mindstorms or Ozobot. These kits allow your child to build and program robots to perform various tasks, combining hands-on learning with coding.
- Minecraft Modding: If your child is a Minecraft fan, consider introducing them to modding. Minecraft modding platforms like "Minecraft: Education Edition" allow your child to modify the game using code.
- Coding with Art: Integrate art and creativity into coding using platforms like Pencil Code or Processing. Children can create visual art and animations while learning to code.

Overall, fourth graders can use valuable life lessons to promote personal growth and prepare them to face the challenges and responsibilities of adolescence and adulthood with competence and confidence. Continue to practice key skills such as critical thinking, problem-solving, and responsibility to reinforce their decision-making skills. Setting a foundation for sound decision-making skills will help them throughout their lives.

Chapter 10

Fifth Grade

Fifth graders are on the cusp of adolescence, navigating away from childhood. They love being one of the big kids on campus. This is a critical stage for personal and social development. Life skills such as emotional regulation, self-awareness, and conflict resolution become increasingly important as children navigate the emotional and social challenges of this age.

A big transitional year from elementary to middle school, it's a time of mixed emotions for them. All they've known has been elementary school, and they may be intimidated by the thought of middle school as it approaches. Next year, they'll be introduced to a more complex educational environment with multiple teachers, changing classrooms, and increased responsibilities. Their life skills help them adapt to the upcoming changes, where they must manage their schedules, stay organized, and communicate effectively with various peers and adults. Here are a few more skills, their benefits, and exercises to add to their repertoire:

Cooking:

Benefits: A practical life skill that promotes independence and self-esteem. Foster a sense of ownership over their food choices. Preparing meals and cleaning up afterward instills a sense of responsibility. Children learn to follow safety rules, handle kitchen tools, and clean up their cooking messes.

Activities:

- Boxed and Frozen Meals: They should have been practicing how to use the microwave and stove with your supervision. They may be able to cook a box of mac n' cheese or heat up a frozen hot pocket if no one is home. Remind them to keep younger siblings away from the kitchen, never leave food cooking unattended, how to fan out a smoke detector for burnt food, show them where you store the fire extinguisher, how to use it, and make it their responsibility to clean up afterward.
- Pop a seal: Opening screw lids can be difficult for adults. Show them the key to easily opening a lid by carefully taking a dull knife under the lid and prying the side until the seal pops. Unscrewing the lid that way is so much easier, but be careful not to stab anything while doing so. There are also grip pads and small appliances made for unscrewing lids.
- Classes: Learn about nutrition or how to cook with classes that teach hands-on, healthy eating. This could be a fun activity with a parent or friends.
- Magazine Subscription: If your child loves to cook, consider paying for a child-friendly magazine subscription from Chopchopfamily.org. They have culturally diverse, easy-to-follow recipes that teach nutrition and kitchen skills geared towards families.

Decision-making skills:

Benefits: Empower your child to take an active role in shaping their lives. They learn that they have the capacity to make choices and influence outcomes. Learn to assess risks and benefits, weighing potential advantages and disadvantages of different options.

Activities:

- Help plan vacations: Where would they like to go? What kind of activities and events are there? Have them plan the logistics, like searching for transportation such as airfare based on price, time, and stops. Come up with a potential list of lodging. Look into popular attractions and search for hidden gems in online and print travel guides.
- Calendar: Prioritize the activities and events based on importance when planning each day, week, and month.
- Shopping: Have them decide how and when to spend their money. Teach the consequences of impulsive shopping vs. delayed gratification. Spend it all now on junk or save for something they really want later.

Emotional Regulation:

Benefits: Reduces emotional outbursts, increases self-control, and improves emotional health. Learning to manage emotions is crucial for mental well-being and positive relationships.

Activities:

- Mindfulness exercises: Show them how to reset with deep breathing or guided meditation. Help them stay present and manage strong emotions.
- Coping Strategies: Teach children to take a break, count to ten, or find a quiet space to calm down from intense emotions.
- Journaling: They can write about their feelings, what triggered them, and how they managed those emotions. What works and what doesn't? Learn from experiences. Journaling provides a healthy outlet for self-expression.
- Positive Self-Talk: Teach them to challenge negative thoughts and replace them with more constructive and optimistic ones. Changing words can help kids begin to make the change from a fixed to a growth mindset. Remove the thought of "I can't." Teach "the power of yet." Popularized by psychologist Carol Dweck, it encourages individuals to view challenges, setbacks, and failures not as

permanent limitations but as opportunities for learning and development. Incorporate positive affirmations with phrases like, "I am smart, kind, and beautiful," and have them repeat these affirmations daily.

- Visualization exercises: Help reduce anxiety and stress by visualizing the potential outcomes of various decisions. Visualize positive results. Many athletes practice this for a winning mindset. If they can dream it, they can achieve it.
- Dealing with death: Whether it be a pet or a person, death is a natural part of life and inevitable. Be honest about what happened, and provide factual information appropriate for their age. Encourage your child to ask questions and express their feelings. Share stories, photos, and memories. Keeping their memory alive can be comforting. Consider creating a small memorial or ritual to remember the person or pet who has passed away. Our family buys flowers when visiting my father's columbarium and pulls out a couple to keep in a vase at home. It's a small way to set an intentional remembrance. Lighting a candle, planting a tree, or making a scrapbook can be meaningful activities. Prepare your child for what to expect at a memorial service. Allow them to decide whether to attend or participate in a funeral or ceremony. Visit a flower shop and have them help choose which arrangement to buy. Recognize that each child may cope with death differently. Some may want to talk and share, while others may need time alone or express their feelings through other means. If your child is struggling to cope with grief, exhibits prolonged signs of distress, or experiences significant changes in behavior, consider seeking the assistance of a grief counselor or therapist who specializes in children's grief.

Home Skills:

Benefits: Helps set responsibilities, expectations, and the importance of cooperation within the household. Prepares children to be more independent.

Activities:

- Changing light bulbs: Teach your child to change a light bulb safely. Make sure the light switch is set to off. Most light bulbs only require a screw in and out. Some bathroom and garage lights need a delicate twist. Have them practice.
- Bathroom Cleaning: Scrubbing the tub and toilet. No one likes to do it, but we all need to know how. Show your child the proper cleaners to use and how to apply pressure when scrubbing. Discuss how often it should be done and have them responsible for cleaning their own bathroom. By now, they should know how to clean the entire bathroom, from mirrors, sinks, and toilets to tubs.
- Making the bed: By now, they should be making their bed every morning. They should also be able to change their sheets.
- Operating a washing machine and dryer: Teach your child to read labels, sort, and load the laundry. Take them to a laundromat to use coin-operated machines or make a drop-off at the dry cleaners. Show them the different settings and how to use cleaners. Measure the correct amount of detergent, fabric softener, and bleach. Remember to spot-check for stains and practice using different stain removers or a soft brush. Remind them that a stain will set once their clothes are heat-dried. Have them check pockets, too. Show them how to decipher delicate clothing and the importance of air drying. Have them use reminders on a device or a visible sheet of paper to switch clean clothes to the dryer and clean the lint trays with each load. It is a good idea to have them turn off the dryer if the house is unoccupied, as electrical fires can start with a dryer, but remember to turn it back on. Having them do their own laundry may prevent the massive loads that come from their room. They may learn to conserve a bit.
- Ironing: Although it's not used as much on clothes, it may come in handy one day. Teach them the importance of being careful around the heat, how to adjust settings based

on the labels, and how to use the steamer. Who knows, a really polished look may come back in style.

- Mowing: If you have grass, now is the time to teach your child how to mow the lawn and make it a part of their chores. Teach and supervise them on how to use the mower, trimmer, and how to tidy up after the mess. If you have dogs, hopefully, your child is accustomed to picking up the doggie diamonds already, so they should be familiar with the yard. Your child might consider perfecting their craft and offering services around the neighborhood to add to their savings. Only really motivated kids will take you up on that offer, though!

Media literacy:

Benefits: Become more critical consumers of information and media content. It is essential for distinguishing between reliable and unreliable sources, understanding media biases, and making informed choices. Develop critical-thinking skills, make informed decisions, recognize different points of view, and become a smart consumer.

Activities:

- Media Sources: Discuss television, websites, social media, and advertisements. Analyze advertisements together, pointing out persuasive techniques, emotional appeals, and the difference between advertising and reality.
- Reliable Sources: Discuss the importance of checking the credibility of information and verifying it with multiple sources. Identify reliable and unreliable media outlets. Practice verifying claims made in news articles or other media posts. Decipher information as "fact," "opinion," and "entertainment."
- Critical Viewing: When watching TV shows, movies, or videos, encourage your child to think critically about the content. Discuss the portrayal of characters, stereotypes, and the potential influence of media on beliefs and behaviors.

- Recognize Bias: Help them understand media bias by discussing how different sources may present information from specific perspectives. Encourage them to consider multiple viewpoints. Have them recognize this when getting advice from people, as well.
- Current Events Discussions: Encourage discussions about current events and news stories. Explore different news sources to see how they cover the same events differently. Many outlets have content directed specifically for kids, such as TIME for Kids, Nightly News: Kids Editions, etc.
- Online Safety: You may not allow your child access to social media, but chances are some of their friends will be active users. Remind your child about online privacy and safety. Discuss the importance of not sharing personal information, especially with strangers, and practicing caution about what gets posted online. Posts are not anonymous; there are trails. Teach them responsible behavior. Undesirable posts could haunt them in the future. Use respectful communication. Recognize potential cyberbullying.
- Set Screen Time Limits and Monitor Activities: It's easy to rely on screen time as a babysitter, but help them promote a healthy balance between screen time and other activities, such as reading, playing outdoors, or spending time with family and friends. If they have online accounts, maintain an open line of communication about their online experiences. Be aware of their online interactions and provide guidance when needed.

Physical:

Benefits: Improves physical fitness, coordination, and overall well-being. Encourage regular physical activity and skill-building exercises. Emphasize the importance of safety, proper warm-ups, and cool-downs.

Activities:

- Outdoor Play: Encourage them to engage in outdoor play activities like playing tag, hide and seek, soccer, basketball, or riding bicycles. These activities promote cardiovascular fitness and coordination.
- Exercise: Help build endurance by working out as a family. Make a training circuit incorporating jumping jacks, jump ropes, sit-ups, and push-ups. Set up obstacle courses in your backyard or at a local park. These can include crawling under tables, climbing over play structures, balancing on a line, and jumping over cones. Make family-friendly competitions!
- Sports and Team Activities: Enroll them in sports teams or clubs at school or in the community. Team sports like soccer, basketball, or baseball help develop teamwork and sportsmanship.
- Dance: Classes or dance-based video games can be a fun way to improve coordination, balance, and flexibility.
- Martial Arts: Martial arts classes can teach discipline, focus, balance, and self-defense skills. Many martial arts schools offer programs for children.
- Hiking: Go on family hikes or nature walks to explore the outdoors while promoting physical activity. This is an excellent activity for clearing their minds and escaping a fixed routine.
- Skating and Rollerblading: A fun way to work on balance and coordination.
- Climbing: Visit a rock climbing gym or climbing wall to build strength and confidence.
- Playground Workouts: Use the playground as a fitness resource. Encourage them to use monkey bars, swings, and other equipment for exercise.

Safety:

Benefits: Make informed decisions and protect themselves in various situations.

Activities:

- Halloween: Supervise them carving a pumpkin for Halloween. Help them plan for a scary decoration in a safe way. Think of the audience in your neighborhood.
- CPR: Take a local lesson to learn CPR and refresh on the Heimlich Maneuver.
- Home Alone: Depending on your child's maturity level, they may be able to stay at home alone for short periods of time. If you feel comfortable, have them watch younger siblings, but make sure they know how to reach you and what to do in case of an emergency. Leave a way for them to call for help.

Study Skills:

Benefits: Helps your child prepare for tests, complete assignments, and become more independent learners.

Activities:

- Note-taking: Help them acquire strategies for retaining information. Highlight key points and use abbreviations. Summarize and review information.
- Study Groups: Encourage group sessions with classmates, which can help them reinforce their understanding of the material and clarify any doubts.
- Tools: Use flashcards, mnemonic devices, and mind maps. Use music, rhymes, and acrostics to enhance memorization skills. Organize information and relationships visually.
- Test-Taking Strategies: Teach your child to read all instructions carefully, budget time effectively, and review answers before submitting. Create sample tests or quizzes for them to build confidence.
- Goal Setting: Help them set academic goals for themselves, whether it's improving grades, completing assignments early, or participating more actively in class.
- Positive Mindset: Foster a positive attitude toward learning and studying. Emphasize that mistakes are part of the learning process and an opportunity for growth.

Technology:

Benefits: Develop skills that are increasingly important in today's digital world. Stay involved in their online activities, set boundaries, and monitor their internet usage to ensure a safe online experience.

Activities:

- Device Proficiency: Ensure your child is comfortable using various devices, including basic functions like powering them on, using a keyboard and mouse, navigating a device, charging batteries, and troubleshooting. Show your child how to restart a device or check for updates. Learn to ask for help.
- Basic Office Programs: If they haven't already been exposed to various office programs online, show your child how emails, word processing, spreadsheets, and presentations differ. Help them create, organize, and find files.
- Typing Skills: Encourage your child to master touch typing through online programs or games. Work to improve typing speed and accuracy can boost their productivity.
- Online Collaboration: Introduce your child to online collaboration tools like Google Workspace to work on projects with classmates.
- Graphic Design: Explore basic graphic design tools and software, such as Canva or Paint, for creating simple graphics and images.
- Holiday Card - Have them help design the card by choosing pictures and a layout. Make a list of recipients. Encourage them to type personal messages or a generic recap of the year to copy and paste. Have them compile email addresses and send them out. Or, if you have the time and patience, do the same, but for physical cards. Have them address the envelopes, purchase stamps, and mail them.
- Calendar and Email: Use an online calendar to stay organized and share relevant events with family. Email family and friends and share images taken together.

- Shopping: Comparison shop for pricing the same items online and in stores. Find alternative options if the item is no longer available or too expensive. Discuss quality and quantity. Smart shopping is easier than ever and will only improve for the tech-savvy.
- Order Food: Order groceries from stores or meals from restaurants. Download money-saving apps.
- Tutorial: Use an online tutorial to learn something new, like how to knit or practice a new trick. Encourage routine use or completion of courses.

Remember that every child is unique, and what works well for one child may not work as effectively for another. Encourage your child to explore different strategies to find what suits them best. The key is to instill a love for learning and equip them with the tools to become independent and motivated best versions of themselves.

Chapter 11

Practice Scenarios

Help your child see the practical application of life skills in their everyday lives. Practice these skills through discussions and role-play. With each scenario, you can change the perspective by replacing your child and people they know instead of using the names below. Some kids prefer to use a third-person viewpoint. You can act the scenarios out with your child or use toys to demonstrate a situation. Brainstorm resolutions with your child. These real-life scenarios can serve as effective teaching tools for illustrating the importance of various life skills in a relatable and practical context for elementary-aged children. By engaging in these situations, kids can gain valuable experience and build the confidence to handle similar challenges as they continue to grow and develop.

Whenever you have some extra time, you can practice a new scenario. That could be daily, once a week, or monthly. To help keep track, you can check them off as you introduce a skill. There are endless options, but here are 65 scenarios that elementary-aged children can relate to, along with the life skills they illustrate:

Sharing Toys

- Life Skills: Empathy and Cooperation
- Set the Scene: Two friends, Alex and Taylor, are playing together. They both want to use the same toy, but there's only one available.
- Lesson: They need to decide how to share it fairly. Consider taking turns. They could play rock, paper, scissors to see who gets to play with the toy first for a set period of time. They might want to play together. Think about how the other child feels and compromise.

Getting Ready for School

- Life Skills: Time Management, Organization and Responsibility
- Set the Scene: Emily needs to prepare for school in the morning. She has a limited amount of time to brush her teeth, get dressed, eat breakfast, and pack her backpack.
- Lesson: Setting a schedule can help with time management. Ensure a smooth start to the day. Consider ways to make more time by getting up earlier, setting out clothes, and packing her school supplies in her backpack the night before. Use a system to track tasks that need to be completed and monitor the time by setting smart alarms.

Dealing with Frustration

- Life Skills: Emotional Regulation and Problem-Solving
- Set the Scene: Liam is trying to build a tower with blocks, but it keeps falling over. He's getting frustrated and needs to figure out how to stabilize it.
- Lesson: He could ask an adult, sibling, or friend for help. Show him how to build a more substantial base and carefully add to the structure.

Resolving a Disagreement

- Life Skills: Communication and Conflict Resolution

- Set the Scene: Two friends, Blake and Josey, are arguing over which game to play during recess. They both want to play their favorite games and refuse to compromise.
- Lesson: Children can learn the importance of resolving conflicts peacefully. They can discover that compromise, active listening, and understanding the feelings of others are essential for maintaining friendships. They could take turns so they can both have fun.

Taking Care of a Pet

- Life Skills: Responsibility and Empathy
- Set the Scene: Sarah has a pet hamster named Whiskers. She needs to remember to feed him, clean his cage, and give him attention to make sure he's happy and healthy.
- Lesson: This scenario teaches children about the responsibilities associated with pet ownership. It emphasizes the importance of caring for their pets' needs and being reliable in fulfilling their duties. She will develop empathy by understanding the pet's needs and feelings.

Making Healthy Food Choices

- Life Skills: Healthy Eating Habits and Decision-Making
- Set the Scene: It's lunchtime, and Ethan has to choose between a sandwich with fruits or a bag of chips. He needs to decide what will be the best option for his health.
- Lesson: He could choose the fruits, and if he's still hungry, have the chips. It's best to choose healthier options and have a balanced meal. If he has a choice, maybe choosing dried apple chips can be the best of both worlds.

Dealing with a Lost Item

- Life Skills: Problem-solving, Adaptability, and Resilience
- Set the Scene: Olivia can't find her favorite toy.

- Lesson: By being better organized, she could find her toys more easily. She needs to think about where she last saw it and look in different places to try to find it. She could ask for help in finding the toy. She can not give up until she finds it.

Standing Up to Bullying

- Life Skills: Assertiveness and Empathy
- Set the Scene: Alex sees a classmate being teased by others.
- Lesson: He could try pulling his friend away from the situation by calling him over. He could stick up for his friend. He needs to find a way to support his classmate, and if the situation persists, let an adult know. He knows when to ask a trusted adult to address the situation.

Getting Ready for Bed

- Life Skills: Self-Care and Healthy Hygiene
- Set the Scene: Emma needs to brush her teeth, wash her face, and put on her pajamas before going to bed.
- Lesson: She needs to know these routines help her stay healthy. She could make a chart to remind her what needs to be done.

Planning a Playdate

- Life Skills: Organization and Communication
- Set the Scene: Lily wants to have a playdate with her friend, Max.
- Lesson: Plan out what needs to be done to have a playdate. She needs to talk to her parents about it, find a time that works for both families and plan some activities they can do together.

Working on a Project

- Life Skills: Time Management

- Set the Scene: Daniel has a school project due in a week, but he keeps procrastinating and spends most of his time playing video games. As the deadline approaches, he becomes stressed.
- Lesson: Children can understand the significance of managing their time wisely and prioritizing tasks. They can learn that procrastination can add to stress and that breaking tasks into smaller, manageable parts can help. Perhaps use a planner to stay on top of the task and work on the project a little bit each day.

Washing Up

- Life Skills: Healthy Hygiene
- Set the Scene: Sarah has been playing outside all day, and she comes home covered in dirt. She refuses to wash her hands before dinner and goes straight to the table.
- Lesson: This scenario illustrates the importance of maintaining good hygiene practices, especially before eating. Children can learn that washing their hands helps avoid the spread of germs and keeps them healthy. Practice washing hands for at least 20 seconds to prevent germs.

Working Together

- Life Skills: Collaboration and Teamwork
- Set the Scene: During a class project, Lucy and her classmates need to build a cardboard castle. Lucy wants to do everything herself because she thinks her ideas are the best.
- Lesson: This scenario emphasizes the value of working collaboratively with others. Children can learn that sharing ideas, listening to others, and working as a team can lead to better results and a more enjoyable experience.

Being Supportive

- Life Skills: Empathy
- Set the Scene: Mark notices that his friend, Lily, is feels because she failed a test. Instead of making fun of her, he sits with her and offers words of encouragement.
- Lesson: This scenario demonstrates the importance of empathy and understanding the feelings of others. Children can learn that showing kindness and support to friends who are going through tough times is a valuable skill. Golden Rule: Treat others how you'd like to be treated.

Difficult Decisions

- Life Skills: Decision Making
- Set the Scene: Emma has a difficult choice to make. She has to decide between attending a birthday party or helping her family with a community cleanup event happening on the same day.
- Lesson: In this scenario, children can grasp the concept of making choices and weighing the pros and cons. They can learn that decision-making involves considering their priorities and values.

Presentation Panic

- Life Skills: Planning, Emotional Regulation, Mindfulness
- Set the Scene: David feels very nervous about giving a presentation in front of his class.
- Lesson: David learns the importance of recognizing and managing his emotions. He practices techniques to deal with anxiety and stress in a healthy way. David practices deep breathing and positive self-talk to calm his nerves. He practices his speech, uses visual aids, and builds confidence in public speaking.

Watching TV

- Life Skills: Communication and Conflict Resolution

- Set the Scene: Two siblings, Alex and Mia, have a disagreement about which TV show to watch.
- Lesson: The children can practice expressing their thoughts and feelings calmly. Find a compromise, like taking turns choosing a show they both like.

Preparing a Simple Snack

- Life Skills: Independence and Responsibility
- Set the Scene: A child, Max, wants a snack but needs help making a sandwich.
- Lesson: Max can learn to make a simple sandwich with parental guidance and be responsible for cleaning up after making the snack.

Welcoming a New Student

- Life Skills: Empathy and Collaboration
- Set the Scene: A new student, Maya, joins the class, and Sally wants to make her feel welcome.
- Lesson: Sally can empathize with Maya's situation and introduce her to the class. She could include her in activities.

Gaming vs. Homework

- Life Skills: Decision-Making and Time Management
- Set the Scene: Daniel wants to play on his Switch but hasn't finished his homework.
- Lesson: Daniel needs to prioritize what's important and manage his time effectively to balance various activities.

Setting the Table

- Life Skills: Responsibility and Collaboration
- Set the Scene: Sarah's family is having dinner, and she's responsible for setting the table.

- Lesson: She needs to ensure there are enough plates, utensils, and glasses for everyone. If she doesn't know where to place them, ask for help with the first setting. She can use that setting as an example for completing the rest on her own.

Planning a Family Outing

- Life Skills: Decision-Making and Collaboration
- Set the Scene: The Johnson family wants to plan a weekend outing.
- Lesson: Each family member can be assigned a task or team up to work on the planning together. They need to decide on a destination, activities, and a budget that works for everyone.

Handling Peer Pressure

- Life Skills: Assertiveness and Critical Thinking
- Description: Kate's friends want her to do something she knows is wrong.
- Lesson: She needs to stand up for her values, say no, and make the right choice.

Saving Money for a Special Toy

- Life Skills: Financial Literacy and Goal Setting
- Set the Scene: Jake really wants to buy a particular toy, but it's expensive.
- Lesson: He needs to figure out how to save his allowance, set a budget, and be patient as he works toward his goal.

Planning a School Project

- Life Skills: Time Management and Organization
- Set the Scene: Mia and Lucas have a school project due in a few weeks.

- Lesson: They must plan their research, gather materials, and work together to complete the project on time.

Expressing Gratitude

- Life Skills: Empathy and Communication
- Set the Scene: After receiving a thoughtful gift, Emma must thank the person who gave her the gift.
- Lesson: She could write a note to show her appreciation and practice expressing gratitude.

Handling Online Safety

- Life Skills: Technology Skills and Safety Awareness
- Set the Scene: Ben is playing an online game at his friend's house. Someone they don't know sends him an online message. He seems friendly and nice.
- Lesson: He needs to remember Stranger Danger. Don't interact or share personal information with strangers.

Preparing for a Rainy Day

- Life Skills: Adaptability and Problem-Solving
- Set the Scene: Evie and Lily planned to go to the park, but it's raining.
- Lesson: They must adapt their plans and create indoor activities to enjoy together.

Managing Homework

- Life Skills: Time Management and Organization
- Set the Scene: Emily has multiple homework assignments due this week.
- Lesson: She needs to create a schedule, prioritize tasks, and break them into manageable parts to complete them on time.

Respecting Personal Boundaries

- Life Skills: Empathy and Respect
- Set the Scene: Jack wants to play with his friend, Madison, but she needs some alone time.
- Lesson: Jack learns to respect Madison's boundaries and waits for her to be ready to play. He finds something else to do in the meantime and doesn't take it personally.

Handling a Lost Tooth

- Life Skills: Healthy Hygiene and Adaptability
- Setting the Scene: Bradley loses a tooth unexpectedly at school.
- Lesson: If he's at school, he might ask to see the school nurse. Stay calm, and use a clean tissue or gauze to soak up any blood. Put the tooth somewhere safe so that he can show it to his parents. He'll want to clean it and place it somewhere for the Tooth Fairy later that night.

Emergency Preparedness

- Life Skills: Safety Awareness and Critical Thinking
- Set the Scene: A sudden power outage occurs while Alex is home alone.
- Lesson: Alex knows where the emergency supplies are kept, finds a flashlight, entertains his younger siblings with a card game, and stays safe until the lights come back on or his parents return.

Supporting a Friend in Need

- Life Skills: Empathy and Emotional Intelligence
- Set the Scene: Zoe's friend, Ethan, is feeling sad.
- Lesson: She uses her listening skills, offers comfort, and encourages him to talk about his feelings, helping him feel better.

Making a Simple Meal

- Life Skills: Basic Cooking Skills and Independence
- Set the Scene: Henry wants to make a peanut butter and jelly sandwich for himself.
- Lesson: He learns how to handle kitchen tools safely and follows simple instructions to prepare his meal.

Managing Screen Time

- Life Skills: Technology Skills and Self-Control
- Set the Scene: Sophie enjoys playing video games but realizes she's been playing for a long time.
- Lesson: She practices self-control by setting a timer to limit her screen time. Then, she finds something else to do, like read, draw, or play with her toys.

Handling a Lost Pet

- Life Skills: Empathy, Problem-Solving, and Resilience
- Set the Scene: Lyla's cat goes missing.
- Lesson: She searches for her pet, puts up "Lost Cat" signs, and asks neighbors for help, demonstrating determination.

Planning a Garden

- Life Skills: Planning and Patience
- Setting the Scene: Daniel and Willow want to grow a garden.
- Lesson: They plan the layout, choose plants, and patiently care for their garden as it grows over time. They take turns watering, weeding, and harvesting the plants together.

Time for Exercise

- Life Skills: Goal Setting and Self-Discipline
- Description: Kai wants to become better at hula.

- Lesson: She sets a goal to practice for 20 minutes daily, demonstrating self-discipline and determination.

Preparing for a Family Picnic

- Life Skills: Planning and Goal Setting
- Set the Scene: Steve wants to go on a family picnic.
- Lesson: He checks the weather. He asks his family for available dates and locks in a time. Steve decides on the menu and makes a grocery list. He goes grocery shopping with his parents, and on the day, he packs the supplies, and they all have a wonderful time bonding. Way to go, Steve!

Respecting Differences

- Life Skills: Empathy and Respect for Diversity
- Sets the Scene: At school, Casey meets a new student from a different country.
- Lesson: She befriends the new student, learns about their culture, and demonstrates respect for differences.

Popup Screen

- Life Skills: Online Safety and Critical Thinking
- Set the Scene: Charles sees a suspicious popup screen telling him to click on it while playing an online game.
- Lesson: He remembers what he learned about online safety and doesn't click on any links. He also ignores anything that asks to be purchased and knows not to share any personal information.

Building a Birdhouse

- Life Skills: Creativity and DIY Skills
- Set the Scene: Michelle and Mitch decide to build a birdhouse.

- Lesson: They find a tutorial online or in a book. They follow instructions, use tools safely, and express their creativity through this DIY project.

Sharing with a New Sibling

- Life Skills: Responsibility, Patience, Empathy and Sharing
- Set the Scene: Payton becomes a big sister and needs to share her toys and parents' attention with her new sibling.
- Lesson: She carefully watches her parents care for her sister and offers to help. Payton helps feed her, changes diapers, and plays with her. She loves her little sister.

Helping a Neighbor

- Life Skill: Social, Kindness, and Community Involvement
- Set the Scene: Nathan notices his elderly neighbors haven't shoveled their driveway or walkways for several days. Another snowstorm is on its way.
- Lesson: With his parents' permission, he offers to help, demonstrating kindness, and a sense of community. They take him up on the offer and he is brimming with feel-good vibes. They offer him money to do it for the next snowfall.

Resolving a Misunderstanding

- Life Skills: Communication and Empathy
- Setting the Scene: Karen has a misunderstanding with her sister, Kim.
- Lesson: They sit down together, talk about their feelings, and work together to resolve the issue.

Participating in a Team Sport

- Life Skills: Collaboration and Sportsmanship
- Set the Scene: Colton wants to play football. He joins a flag football team.

- Lesson: He learns to work with his teammates, celebrate their successes, and handle losses with good sportsmanship.

Navigating Public Transportation

- Life Skills: Independence and Problem-Solving
- Set the Scene: Emi and her mom want to go sightseeing in a new country while on vacation.
- Lesson: Emi learns how to read a local train schedule, researches the best passes to purchase, plans their routes, and navigates public transportation safely.

Creating a Savings Goal

- Life Skills: Financial Literacy and Goal Setting
- Set the Scene: Jake wants to buy a new bicycle.
- Lesson: He sets a savings goal, opens a bank account, and learns to save a portion of his weekly allowance. Jake resists impulse purchases and patiently saves for his bike.

Planning a Family Vacation

- Life Skills: Planning and Budgeting
- Set the Scene: The Francis family wants to go on a vacation.
- Lesson: They decide on a destination, create a budget, and discuss activities they can do together on their trip. They have a fantastic vacation and create a lifetime of memories.

A Weekly Family Game Night

- Life Skills: Planning and Organizing
- Set the Scene: The Smith family decides to have a weekly game night.
- Lesson: Each family member chooses a game, schedules the night, and enjoys quality time together.

Volunteering at an Orphanage

- Life Skills: Organizing, Planning, and Community Service
- Set the Scene: Kellen and Presley spend a day volunteering at an orphanage while on vacation overseas.
- Lesson: Before leaving their home, with the help of their parents, they organized a donation event online for the upcoming visit. The kids spent time planning activities, preparing small gifts based on their needs, and spent quality time sharing experiences with the other children.

Responding to a First Aid Emergency

- Life Skills: First Aid and Quick Thinking
- Set the Scene: While playing at the park, Emily's friend gets a minor injury.
- Lesson: Emily remembers her basic first aid training and helps her friend until an adult arrives.

Organizing a Cookie Sale

- Life Skills: Community Engagement and Teamwork
- Set the Scene: Katie and her friends decide to organize a cookie sale to raise money for their scouting troop.
- Lesson: They work together to plan and run events in their local neighborhood. They also make sure to include calls to their family members because they love cookies and are so supportive!

The Death of a Pet

- Life Skills: Empathy and Responsibility
- Set the Scene: Jackie's pet fish has been floating for too long in the fish tank.
- Lesson: Be honest and age-appropriate. Involve your child in some sort of funeral service. Have them share their emotions and answer any questions they may have.

Planning a Family Birthday Party

- Life Skills: Event Planning and Organization
- Set the Scene: The family is organizing a birthday party for their grandpa.
- Lesson: Help plan a family guest list, decorations, and activities to make it a special day. Brainstorm thoughtful gifts he might like. This might be tough for a guy that has everything. Consider an experience.

Lost at the Park

- Life Skills: Problem-Solving and Decision-Making
- Set the Scene: Johnny can't find his parents at the park.
- Lesson: He needs to stay calm and find a park employee, a police officer, or a mom with kids to get help. Tell them important information like his name, his parents' name, where he was last time he was with his parents, and his phone number.

Setting Up a Lemonade Stand

- Life Skills: Entrepreneurship and Money Management
- Setting the Scene: Chole and Dillon decide to set up a lemonade stand.
- Lesson: They make a plan, calculate costs, make lemonade, buy supplies, set prices, and handle money transactions. Practice service with a smile!

Handling a Broken Toy

- Life Skills: Emotional Regulation, Resilience and Resourcefulness
- Setting the Scene: Frankie finds her favorite toy broken.
- Lesson: She feels upset but is determined to repair it. She asks her parents to help super glue it back together, demonstrating resilience and resourcefulness.

Comforting a Scared Pet

- Life Skills: Empathy and Compassion
- Setting the Scene: Quin's dog is scared during a thunderstorm.
- Lesson: She comforts her pet, providing a safe and soothing environment.

Making a Birthday Card

- Life Skills: Creativity and Attention to Detail
- Setting the Scene: Mia wants to make a special birthday card for her friend.
- Lesson: She uses her creativity to design a unique card, pays attention to details, and adds a personal touch.

Planning a Family Bike Ride

- Life Skills: Planning and Collaboration
- Setting the Scene: Max plans a bike ride with his family.
- Lesson: He decides on a route, helps his parents check the bikes for safety, and enjoys a day of outdoor activity and fun.

Organizing a Family Recycling Program

- Life Skills: Environmental Responsibility and Leadership
- Setting the Scene: Luke asks his family to start a recycling program at home.
- Lesson: He reminds each family member to be mindful in sorting recyclables. With his parents' help, he takes the cans to a recycling center and earns money to put in his bank.

Organizing a Bedroom

- Life Skills: Organization and Cleaning
- Setting the Scene: Wyatt's room is cluttered with toys and clothes.

- Lesson: He organizes his space, putting items in their proper places to create a tidier environment. He shoots his dirty clothes into the laundry bin, puts away his clean clothes, and makes his bed.

Lost Library Book

- Life Skills: Responsibility, Resourcefulness and Communication
- Setting the Scene: Sam borrowed a library book and can't find it anywhere.
- Lesson: He needs to talk to the librarian, explain the situation, and work on a solution to replace the lost book.

Creating Handmade Gifts for Family

- Life Skills: Creativity and Thoughtfulness
- Setting the Scene: Zoe and Maverick decide to make handmade gifts for family members.
- Lesson: They craft personalized gifts, adding a special touch to show their love and appreciation.

Chapter 12

Promotion

During the elementary years, a bigger world picture unfolds with new authority figures, more friends, and experiences. There is a progression from adult-led learning to more independent learning as time goes on. Kids go into elementary school still needing a lot of guidance and end with the beginnings of puberty. That's a lot of changes for kids and parents to go through in a few years!

Ask yourself what you are trying to teach, why it's important, and how to teach it. Depending on the needs of your child, even after leading by example, charts can be a useful tool in displaying instructions providing additional guidance to your child until the skills become second nature. You can use visual charts with pictures to start and progress towards reading words.

Skills develop over time with more experience. A solid foundation of early skills allows for a stable base of building blocks for more complex skills as abilities increase. Along with practicing new skills, your child will gradually become more independent.

Use your child's daily routines to teach life skills, reinforce through play and physical activities, and build positive mental health. For the formative years, the importance of play can not be emphasized enough. Play-based activities teach skills in patience, problem-solving, social skills, and creativity.

Kids need a lot of physical activity. Keeping kids active sets the groundwork for staying fit and helps promote a healthy lifestyle. Learning sports and eventually playing on teams teaches kids to set goals, meet challenges, be resilient, the value of practice for improvement of skills, and teamwork through sportsmanship.

Building a foundation for mental health helps with adversity and stronger relationships. Try keeping your kids away from social media and the internet. Legally (COPPA 1998), children are not allowed to have social media accounts until the age of 13. Studies have found that social media use has strong links to depression due to peer pressure, comparisons, and addictive behavior. If you do give your kids devices, make sure to use the parental controls, monitor their use, and do not allow them to keep their devices in their room overnight. There's really no need to have access once they are asleep.

The theory of out of sight, out of mind works with TV's, too. Try to keep a TV out of your child's bedroom. You may even want to eliminate TV use during the weekdays, or set limits for screen times. A little bit of boredom allows your child to use their imagination and gives time for them to have more active play, which helps them grow mentally and physically.

Encourage your child to share their thoughts, questions, and concerns. Provide age-appropriate explanations. By integrating play, physical activities, and mental health discussions into learning life skills, you can make the learning experience enjoyable, memorable, and beneficial for your child's overall development.

Some of the skills can be mastered early on, but many of the skills outlined in this book will require continued practice over a lifetime. Younger kids are still developing situational awareness of their environment and figuring out how they fit in the world around them. How should they dress based on the weather? How do they clean their room? Who can they trust? Adjust to practice skill for their current and future goals. No matter how much they practice, things may not go their way. Help them learn patience and the value of having a positive mindset to build resilience in adversity. Try to avoid procrastination and the stress associated with it by developing responsible routines and proactive decision-making skills.

During the later years of elementary school, kids will be trying to fit in with their peers and noticing more what makes them like other kids or different. They are becoming more independent, relying less on their parents, and caring more about their friends. Help your child navigate their moral compass and cultivate healthy friendships. Build their belief in themselves and their abilities. Confidence and kindness are critical skills for kids entering the more judgemental years. Children who feel good about themselves are more able to resist negative peer pressure making better choices. They will have a strong mental game for any bullies they may come across.

Transitioning to middle school is undoubtedly a significant milestone in a child's life, filled with new challenges and exciting opportunities. It's a time when the lessons learned in elementary school are put to the test, and the skills honed in the earlier years become invaluable tools. Ready for middle school?!

Here's a checklist to mark off skills introduced and practiced during elementary :

Lower Elementary(Grades K-2)

- Can swim and understands water safety
- Rides a two-wheeled bike with a helmet
- Can fly a kite
- Shows self-esteem
- Expresses feelings, regulates emotions
- Bucket filler
- Has interests
- Communicates verbally and non-verbally
- Pays attention
- Shows manners when speaking, listening, eating, playing, etc.
- Shows gratitude
- Practices phone etiquette

- Follow directions
- Follows rules
- Interacts with others and plays cooperatively
- Plays games (finishes board games)
- Use spatial relationships with others and objects
- Understand cause and effect
- Knows when and how to ask for help
- Helps pack for an overnight stay
- Appropriately respond to others
- Works independently
- Communicates via letter/email/phone calls
- Can complete an assortment of easy puzzles
- Helps care for pets
- Knows proper use of utensils
- Undresses and dresses self according to the weather
- Practices good hygiene
- Completes morning and evening routines
- Showers independently
- Can dry hair with assistance
- Dresses themselves
- Demonstrates time management
- Can state name, age, and gender upon request
- Attempt to pour and stir
- Sets and clears the table
- Prepares snacks
- Helps prepare non-cooked meals
- Properly stores food
- Begin to understand the use of money
- Understands needs vs. wants
- Demonstrates safety
- Knows Stranger Danger and can identify inappropriate touches
- Understands Stop, Drop & Roll
- Understands Slip, Slop & Slap
- Can administer basic first aid
- Knows what to do in an emergency
- Basic sewing

- Setting and achieving short-term goals
- Reads daily
- Can tell time
- Completes homework
- Helps with laundry
- Cleans own room and makes bed
- Physical activity for at least an hour a day
- Reduces, reuses & recycles
- Completes basic household chores
- Knows proper battery usage and how to change them out
- Uses technology for learning
- Safe online practices

Upper Elementary (Grades 3-5)

- Shows self-confidence
- Takes care of their nails
- Styles hair
- Understands the physical and emotional changes of puberty
- Uses coping strategies
- Use active listening skills
- Communicates ideas
- Can sign their name
- Practices polite refusal skills
- Respects others
- Uses "I" statements
- Problem-solves and conflict-resolves
- Has a sleepover
- Helps pack a suitcase for a vacation
- Gardens
- Volunteers
- Can do basic household repairs
- Use simple common tools independently, such as paper punch and screwdriver
- Knows how to safely operate kitchen appliances (blender, microwave, stove, oven, dishwasher, etc).
- Operates washer and dryer

- Mows and tidies up the yard
- Cleans their entire bathroom
- Prepares simple cooked meals for themselves
- Follows recipes
- Understand food and clothing labels
- Deciphers the value of money
- Can calculate change
- Purchases thoughtful gifts and wraps them
- Sends "Thank you" notes
- Knows their address and phone number
- Navigates with a GPS and physical map
- Setting and achieving long-term goals
- Comprehends reading
- Completes projects
- Organizes school supplies and learning area
- Uses a planner and prioritizes tasks
- Plays sports or recreational activities
- Cares for garden or pet
- Grooms themselves
- Can change light bulbs
- Uses apps to make orders
- Touch types
- Understands how to use basic office programs
- Uses study strategies

Chapter 13

Conclusion

"**The days are long, but the years are short**" is often attributed to Gretchen Rubin, a well-known author and happiness expert. The quote has resonated with many parents, highlighting the paradoxical nature of time perception, especially in the context of raising children. It's a poignant reminder of how quickly time passes, especially in the journey of parenthood. While the daily challenges and demands of raising children can sometimes make the hours feel never-ending, the years seem to slip by in the blink of an eye. Even in the midst of chaos, cherish the moments because childhood is fleeting. Savor the precious moments with your child and make the most of your time with them as they grow and change quickly, moving on to new chapters in their lives.

The elementary school years will pass before you know it. With each passing year, your child will be less reliant on you and increasingly more independent. Cherish the time you have with your little ones. While teaching our kids important life skills and gaining academic knowledge is undeniably essential, it's equally crucial to remember that the time we spend with our children and the memories we create are invaluable. These moments of connection, laughter, and shared experiences shape our children in profound ways. By investing quality time with our kids, we not only foster a strong parent-child bond but also provide a safe and nurturing environment for them to learn, grow, and flourish. These lasting memories become the building blocks of their self-esteem and resilience, guiding them as they navigate life's challenges and develop into well-rounded, confident individuals. In the hustle and bustle of daily life, it's these cherished moments that become the heart of a loving and supportive family, enriching our children's lives, instilling values, and nurturing a deep sense of belonging. These memories become the foundation upon which they build their own lives, forming a reservoir of strength and support they can always draw upon.

As we come to the final chapter of this guide, I hope you've found inspiration and reassurance in the incredible growth and development your child has made. Through the pages of this life skills book, we've seen the transformation of a hesitant kindergartener into a confident and capable fifth grader, ready to take on the challenges of middle school. We've explored a range of skills, from communication and problem-solving to empathy and time management, and witnessed how they are all interconnected.

Communication: The Foundation of Connection

Communication is the cornerstone of relationships and understanding. Your child can convey thoughts, listen actively, and connect with peers, teachers, and the world around them. In middle school, this skill will be their bridge to forming new friendships, seeking help when needed, and sharing their thoughts and ideas with confidence.

Problem-Solving: Unleashing Creativity

Your child's journey from simple puzzles to tackling complex equations showcases their remarkable problem-solving abilities. They've learned to approach challenges with creativity, resilience, and a determination to find solutions. As they enter middle school, they'll face various issues – from complex homework assignments to peer conflicts. But they are equipped with the tools to dissect issues, consider multiple perspectives, and find innovative solutions.

Decision Making: Charting Their Path

Decision-making, what started as a decision on what to wear every day, has now evolved into a skill that guides your child's journey into middle school. With a myriad of choices from elective courses to extracurricular activities, your child can weigh options, consider consequences, and make informed decisions, and is well-prepared to chart a path that aligns with their passions and interests.

Empathy: Building Connections

Empathy, the ability to understand and share the feelings of others, has transformed your child into a compassionate friend and a source of support for their peers. Middle school can be an emotional roller-coaster, but your child's empathetic nature will be a beacon of comfort and understanding, helping them form meaningful connections with classmates and offering solace during challenging times.

Emotional Intelligence: Mastering Emotions

Emotional intelligence, a skill your child has cultivated over the years, enables them to navigate their own emotions with grace and maturity. In the turbulence of middle school, where emotions can run high, your child can better manage the ups and downs of adolescence.

Time Management: The Key to Balance

Balancing school, activities, and personal time is a skill your child started developing early on. Their ability to prioritize and use time efficiently will serve them well. Middle school schedules can be demanding, but your child's ability to create routines, set priorities, and manage their time effectively will help them excel while maintaining a healthy work-life balance.

Collaboration: Fostering Teamwork

From group activities to resolving conflicts, your child has become a true team player. Their collaborative spirit will be a tremendous asset in the group projects and team activities that await them in middle school. They will work alongside peers on various assignments, and their ability to communicate, compromise, and contribute will make them an invaluable asset to their teams.

Adaptability: Embracing Change

Navigating the transitions from one grade to the next has prepared them to embrace change with open arms. Middle school will introduce them to new teachers, classmates, and routines, but your child's resilience and flexibility will enable them to thrive in this ever-evolving environment.

Self-Confidence: Believing in Themselves

Self-confidence, once a fragile bud, has blossomed into a vibrant flower within your child's heart. They're no longer afraid to raise their hand in class, take on leadership roles in clubs, or face challenges head-on. They've learned that mistakes are opportunities for learning and that confidence comes from embracing challenges. In middle school, this self-assuredness will empower them to pursue their dreams and aspirations with belief in their abilities.

Critical Thinking: A Lifelong Skill

Critical thinking, fostered through explorative play and thought-provoking discussions, has become a lifelong skill that equips your child to analyze information, make informed decisions, and question the world around them. Middle school will present complex ideas and concepts, but your child's critical thinking abilities will enable them to grasp, question, and apply knowledge effectively.

Healthy Hygiene: The Foundation of Well-Being

Healthy hygiene has been instilled through daily routines and habits. In middle school, they will continue to prioritize personal hygiene and recognize its role in maintaining good health and overall well-being. This commitment will ensure they have the energy and focus they need to excel in middle school.

Physical Training: A Lifelong Commitment

Physical training, once a collection of playful activities, has evolved into regular physical activity and a healthy lifestyle. Your child understands the importance of staying active and eating well, which will serve them well in middle school and beyond as they navigate the physical and emotional changes of adolescence.

As you reflect on these skills and the journey your child has taken to develop them, I encourage you to celebrate their growth and readiness for the challenges and adventures that await them in middle school. Your support and guidance have played an integral role in nurturing these skills, and your child is now poised to thrive in the next chapter of their academic and personal journey.

Middle school may hold its share of uncertainties and surprises, but with a strong foundation in these life skills, your child is not only prepared but also empowered to make the most of this exciting phase. As parents, you can take pride in the confident, compassionate, and capable individual your child has become. There will be challenges, and there will be triumphs. Through it all, your child's foundation in these life skills will serve as a steadfast anchor.

So, as your child embarks on this new adventure, remember they are well-equipped, resilient, and ready to shine. Middle school is just the next stepping stone on their remarkable journey of growth and learning, and I have no doubt they will continue to make you proud. I wish you and your child all the best as you embrace the upcoming challenges and celebrate the achievements that lie ahead.

Your child's story is just beginning, and it's bound to be filled with many more chapters of growth and discovery. They are not only prepared; they are poised for success. Their future is bright, and their potential is boundless. As they set forth, armed with these skills, they do so with the knowledge that they are capable of not only facing the world but also shaping it.

If you enjoyed this book, please consider leaving a review on Amazon.com. There, you will find my books on life skills for middle school, high school, college years, and beyond.